Iva Mae:
The Book of
Mom

ROBIN ANNE GRIFFITHS

Iva Mae: The Book of Mom

Robin Anne Griffiths

ISBN-13: 978-0692885499

Chapter 1

After all the years of planning and changing her own funeral arrangements, she was gone. Robin sat in her home office in what felt like the aftermath of a long hard journey. She was thinking back on Iva Mae's life, and found it hard to believe her mother would only be in her memories from now on.

Iva Mae had been planning her own funeral since Robin was a

child. No one really knew why she was so obsessed with the details, but it was a regular topic of conversation, especially as she grew older. Robin and Sandy, her older sister, made fun of it, and it became a regular joke between them and their youngest sister, Tammy. At ninety-one, Iva Mae had finally gone to meet her maker, and the family put together the pieces of the plans that had been made over the years. Robin believed they had done a good job under the circumstances. She also believed that although her mother would have been pleased, she would have been a little disappointed as well.

Over the years, Iva Mae's funeral plans had ranged from a chicken dinner picnic at the cemetery with her favorite gospel singer of the moment to her being flown first class from her final home in Fort Worth to the small cemetery near where she grew up on a farm outside Labette City, Kansas, which had fewer than a hundred people. Iva Mae envisioned all her friends and family arriving for the preaching: it would be her last chance to have all the sinners in her life saved.

Iva Mae had not been an easy person. As Robin went through her mother's personal items, she started to piece together a life filled with family, needs, sorrow, and happiness. It all began in 1922, on the farm in Labette County. Looking at Iva Mae's long life, Robin was amazed at all the different things her mother had experienced over ninety-one years: so much change, most of which she had accepted without a blink. But regarding the few things she did not accept, there was no room for negotiation.

Iva Mae had shared stories of her life and growing up on the farm with her family. Robin was going through the metal box that held her mother's important papers, such as burial plans, special photos of her with family members, and a brief autobiography. This box of miscellaneous papers had been around a long time. Robin could remember it from childhood. As Iva Mae aged, she made sure that Robin and Sandy always knew where it was and whether anything new had been added or changed. But the contents still were surprising.

Iva Mae's parents wedding photo dated 1897
Top row left to right: Uncle George Sissel, Joseph and Ida
Treadway, Uncle John Sissel, Aunt Kate Steinert-Sissel
Bottom row left to right: Uncle Wilford Sissel, Grandpa
Moses Sissel, Grandma Mary Sissel, Uncle John Sissel,
and Great Grandma Emalene Jones.

Chapter 2

I va Mae was the ninth and youngest child of Joseph Albert Treadway and Ida Margaret Anne Sissel. Iva Mae's paternal grandparents were Edmund Frances (Frank) Tredway (the spelling was changed during Edmund's days) and Ellen Parker. Iva Mae's maternal grandparents were Moses Sissel and Mary Jones. All of Iva Mae's children had copies of what was probably Joseph and Ida's wedding photo from 1897.

In the photo are several members of Iva Mae's family, including a great-great-grandmother, but it is hard to be sure it's a wedding photo since—as was typical of the day—everyone is dressed in dark clothing and nobody is smiling. Looking at the photograph, one can see the family likeness passed from Iva Mae's father to her son, Dennis. Joseph was tall, handsome, and well dressed in a three-piece suit with a tie. Iva Mae's mother was attractive and shorter in height. Names like Moses and Albert were common then and have started to surface again in the last few years as popular children's names.

Joseph and Ida's first three children—Emmett Edward, Mary Ellen, and Lula Fern—were close in age. Then there were three girls who died, two of them as infants. Their names were Alta and Ethel. The third, Alma, was three years old when she developed diphtheria and choked to death. Alma was a beautiful, smart child who had her mother's eyes, which were very attractive. All three are buried with no markers at Jamesville Cemetery in Stone County, Missouri, near the grave of their grandfather Moses Sissel. Iva Mae's parents then had three more children—Raymond Russell; Earl Albert, known to everyone as Pete; and Iva Mae. She was born July 3, 1922, and there were twenty-four years between her oldest brother, Emmett, and herself. It's hard to imagine that Emmett was old enough to have served in World War I. Iva Mae always said she was the last child and treated accordingly. She did not like being the youngest.

Iva Mae was born in an exciting time. World War I had ended, and women had just won the right to vote. The flappers in the Roaring Twenties were setting women's fashion on its head, and a new woman was born who smoked, drank, danced, wore makeup, and took risks. The Volstead Act, a law put into place to implement the Eighteenth Amendment, prohibited the brewing of alcoholic beverages for sale.

Iva Mae talked about her family's life in that area around the time she was born. She said land could cost one hundred dollars per acre; rent was two dollars and seventy-five cents plus electricity, which had only recently become available to farm families such as the Treadways, who did not have it. She also said that most field workers were paid thirty-five cents an hour and worked ten hours a day.

Joseph was born in Harrison, Arkansas, and Ida in Billings, Missouri. Ida was a very pretty woman, according to her daughter.

> Mom wasn't five feet tall, and she had huge eyes and long dark hair that she always wore in a bun. She had a hot temper, too. She didn't believe in drinking, card playing, or cussing. She even was on you if you said the word "Gosh," because it was too close to taking the Lord's name in vain.
>
> She was very jealous of Dad, and she didn't want her girls out of her sight because one of them might get pregnant. During this time it was a terrible thing to get pregnant and not be married.
>
> Mom was also very generous. She would do well for the neighbors and give them anything she had. I really didn't know her well because she was always sick after I was born, and she was already thirty-eight years old when she had me.
>
> She was very religious, but family members said she used

to be a lot of fun, too. They used to go swimming after working in the garden or doing chores around the farm. My mom was a worker. She used to help milk the cows, raise a big garden, help in the fields, and can food for the year, just as most women did on a farm.

She was a wonderful cook. She always prepared a huge meal and my family loved to eat.

Iva Mae's memories of early life were all set on their farm in Labette County outside the town of Labette—or as she called it, Labette City. As she would say, Labette was just a wide place in the road in southeast Kansas. The farm was about a mile from Labette, on a creek of the same name. She described her home as a big old house built out of walnut lumber with a large barn for hay. They had no modern conveniences such as plumbing or electricity. They used outhouses during the day, chamber pots at night, and lanterns for light.

The country was changing during the 1920s, but farm life was slow to follow. When World War I ended, many people moved from rural farming communities to the cities. The decade brought forth ownership of cars, radios, and telephones. The average life expectancy in the United States was about fifty-four years. Everyone had their daily chores to do, and life was not easy for a Kansas farm family. The state of Kansas had been opened to settlement for only forty-six years, during which Labette County had been organized.

Farming in Kansas became focused on wheat, since other types of crops did not succeed. The process of growing and harvesting wheat was labor intensive, and horse- or mule-powered threshers began to be replaced with mechanized threshers that harvested the crops. Farming communities were close-knit and families visited each other, but even more important, they helped each other during the harvest.

Horse-drawn plows were commonly used, and the tractor was still an oddity. In Kansas, they grew winter wheat by planting in early fall so that the wheat roots would grow under the snow during the winter. In the spring, melting snow watered the plants, which began to grow and form heads of grain during the warm weather. Usually by July the heads of grain were mature and the wheat could be harvested. There were many risks involved when growing wheat, many of which were related to the weather. Mother Nature had control over whether it would be a good crop year, and farmers would hope that she didn't go to extremes with too much of anything. The wheat would die if it was too hot, and drown if it was too wet.

Harvesting was hard work and required a large crew. Each member of the threshing crew had a specific job to do once the equipment arrived. A machine called a binder was pulled by a horse, a mule, or a tractor during this era. The binder, a heavy piece of equipment, was a modern wonder at the time. It cut the wheat with a blade called a sickle. Once the wheat was cut, it was carried by canvas and dropped into a bed. When enough straw had been gathered, the pressure triggered the binder mechanism, which caused the twine to thread over the bundle and be tied. Once tied, the bundle was pushed over into a carrier. When the carrier became full, the driver of the binder would stop and push a lever to let the load fall to the ground. The machine was an amazing piece of equipment with the way the twine was threaded automatically.

Once the wheat was harvested, the bundles, called shocks, were stood on end in a group to withstand the weather until it could be processed by the threshing machine. The shocks were loaded into horse-drawn wagons and brought to the threshing machine, which was usually set up where the farmer wanted to have the straw. This machine consisted of many moving parts and was powered by a tractor or steam engine, which was kept at a distance from the thresher because of the concern that sparks from the engine would cause a fire.

Once the steam engine or tractor was belted to the thresher and the equipment was running, the processing would begin. Men would stand on top of the wagon, pitching the shocks into the threshing machine. The bundle feeder had a conveying chain that transported the grain bundles into the threshing machine cylinder, where the grain was separated from the stalks. As the machine separated the grain, a fan removed the chaff and dust. The loose grain was transported into a grain wagon by an elevator on the machine and then put into individual bags or stored by some other method that the farmer preferred. The straw continued through the machine to the rear, where it ended in a fan housing that blew it into the straw stack.

The process was a community event, and entire families were involved. Even the children had duties on the day threshing began, and Iva Mae remembered it fondly:

> When I was a small girl, I would get so excited when the month of June came around and the wheat began to turn golden color. I would see my dad getting the binder out of the shed so they could work on it and repair the canvas. That meant just one thing: it's almost threshing time. Threshing time was such fun for me.
>
> We lived in the country, about a mile from a very small

town called Labette City, Kansas. It had a grocery store, filling station, post office, train depot, two churches, a school, and a half grocery store where everyone loafed around, even the hound dogs. I used to wait there every evening to pick up the evening paper to take home after school. My tender ears would get a lot of good listening.

We had really hot summers. And since there was no electricity, we didn't have fans, iceboxes, or anything else like that to keep us cool. But I still couldn't wait till it was threshing time.

Dad had to cut the wheat, and then they shocked it into piles. Then we had to wait until the thresher was able to get to our farm. The neighbors all helped each other, and the women cooked a big dinner.

Lois, a neighbor girl, and I followed the thresher around to the close neighbors. Our job was to set the tables with plates and keep the tea poured. We also would take water to the men in the fields. We rode the grain wagon, which was pulled by horses. Lois's brother, George, hauled the grain, so he would let us go into Labette City with him every now and then to sell a load. He was quite a character, as was the whole family. Lois's sister, Eva, was my teacher for the first four years of school.

Lois and I made quite a pair. She was six years older than me. She was the first one to tell me the facts of life, except she didn't quite know either. She had buckteeth and was skinny. I remember when she was playing ball and was up to bat, she would swing at it like she was chopping wood.

Well, I was no beauty either. I was tall and fat, because I loved food. And my hair would grow so fast that my bangs were always in my eyes, so I was always trying to peep out from under them to see.

As much as I loved threshing time, my mom and big sister Mary used to dread it. There were about twenty men who would come to help. Everyone prepared the best they could, and then it would start. They would cook on woodstoves, and I mean that was a hot job. Also sometimes they stayed for supper, so the cooking would continue. Just when you got through dinner, you had to start supper. You didn't have iceboxes to keep the food in, so you kept it in the cellar.

We would go to town and get ice for the tea and lemonade. Sometimes we would make homemade ice cream for the workers. They loved to come to our house because my mom was such a good cook. She would fix roast beef, fried chicken—which they would kill, clean, and cut up to fry—homemade bread, vegetables out of the garden, cake, and pie. All that had to be prepared from scratch and cooked. The meal was followed by the ice cream, homemade and cranked in a hand freezer. My job was to sit on the freezer to hold it down while they cranked the handle.

It was a hot job for the men as well, because most of the crops were in the bottom fields of Labette Creek, and Kansas can really get hot. They had a steam thresher machine. Men had hay wagons to go to the field to get the shocks of wheat. There would be men in the field to help put it on the wagons. Then they would move the wheat to the thresher so the wheat would go in the grain wagon and the straw would pile up on the ground. That would be fun, because we could play in the straw after the threshing was over. In the winter the straw was used to make beds for the cattle, chickens, and other farm animals.

At night everyone would be tired, hot, and dirty. It was the children's duty in the mornings to fix a big tub of water in the sun so that by that night, it would be warm. The children were first with bathing, then the ladies, then the men. It was all done outside after dark.

My folks were always glad when threshing was over, but I was sad. That meant it was back to being bored, so I would have to go back to reading and following my brothers.

**Iva Mae's family
From left to right:
Joseph, Iva Mae, Ida, Lula, Pete, Mary, Raymond
and Emmett**

Chapter 3

The 1920s, known as the Roaring Twenties or Jazz Age, saw an economic boom after World War I. Cities were, for the first time, surpassing the population of the rural areas. Four presidents served during the twenties, and the country experienced a period of prohibition, crime, and racial tension toward immigrants. Charles Lindbergh made his famous nonstop Atlantic flight to become a national hero, and for the first time a woman, Gertrude Ederle, completed the swim across the English Channel.

The decade also saw new technology, and the country began to shrink with the growth and popularity of automobiles, radios, and movies. The United States became a consumer society with the beginning of mass production and the availability of items that have become necessities. Life in America was transformed during the 1920s in the urban areas, and changes filtered over into the rural areas. Items such as cigarettes and cosmetics became staples of everyday life. Fresh orange juice became available year-round, and for the first time, consumers could buy ready-made clothing in exact sizes.

The automobile began to have an effect on the countryside and change the landscape. Farmers were actually courted by automobile makers, with marketing campaigns promoting vehicles that would replace horses and were made for country roads. Roads were unpaved, so country people didn't always favor automobiles, which would scare livestock and tear up roads by causing deep ruts. But the automobile became more affordable and gave people a new independence for travel they did not have before.

> When I was five years old, Dad surprised everybody by buying a brand new Chevy. It was black with four doors, and had side curtains for the cold or when it rained. We thought it very snazzy.
>
> We had a very good wheat harvest that summer, so I guess the money was burning a hole in his pocket. That is a common trait among all our family members.
>
> No one knew how to drive. I was five years old, so

driving was out of the question for me. My two brothers, Raymond and Pete, were only ten and eight. And Mom was afraid to ride in a car, let alone drive. So that left my big sister Mary, who was twenty-five, and Dad in his fifties.

The man who sold us the car came to show them how to drive. Neither Mary nor Dad really learned, but we had some good experiences. Back then you didn't have to have a driver's license or take any test.

We were really proud of the new car because we didn't have to crank it. Most cars back then had to be cranked to start. The car didn't have a heater, so in winter we wrapped up in blankets, which was still better than being in a horse and wagon. We got there quicker, and we had the side curtains to keep out the cold air.

The roads were dirt, and when it rained in Kansas, you drove in the mud and often got stuck. Then when it dried, there were big ruts in the road. One time Mary came to school to get me and my brothers. The roads were mostly dry but had these big ruts. We were driving in one set of ruts, and my brother Pete said, "Mary, I think those other ruts are better." Behold, she just jumps out of the ruts, but we didn't land in the other ruts. We landed in the ditch, so guess what we had to do? Walk home, so that Dad could come back with the horses and pull us out of the ditch.

Dad always drove on the wrong side of the road. I remember him running over a pig one Christmas going to Parsons. Many times he would forget he was driving the car and think he had the horses and begin yelling, "Whoa, horse. Whoa, horse." Anyway, we parked the car in a shed in the barn and Dad was always forgetting he had the car and would begin to yell "Whoa." But the old Chevy didn't know enough to stop and would go right through the shed. Dad spent half his time repairing the shed when he would go through and not stop.

That car really made life better, especially because we drove to church at night and didn't have to walk home afterwards. I used to get awfully sleepy before I would get home. We didn't have to always walk home from school. We could also drive to Oswego, which was about six miles away. We thought Oswego was a city because it had a movie theater, bank, and library.

We went nearly every Saturday afternoon to Oswego to take the cream and eggs to town and buy groceries. In Oswego, we could get bananas and other food that we could not buy in Labette City. Back then you gave your list to a clerk and they filled your order while you waited. My brothers and I went to the ten-cent western show while my folks did the grocery trading and visited with neighbors.

Then on Sunday, when my sister and brother and their family visited us from Parsons, all my nieces and nephews along with my brothers and I would play cowboys and Indians with our rubber guns.

Before we came home from Oswego, Dad and Mom usually brought us a dime hamburger and five-cent ice cream cone. We weren't rich, but if our folks had any money, we got our share.

I remember when Mary drove the car to Oswego. She couldn't back up, so we would have to find a place to park so she wouldn't have to back the car.

That old Chevy was really a good old car and Dad didn't even have to buy new tires until the boys got old enough to drive. They started to drive at about twelve or thirteen years old, and they really put that car through the mill. The folks would let them take it to Labette to go with someone else, but they never stopped there, so they wore out our new Chevy by the time I was around twelve. I never did get to drive it.

ROBIN ANNE GRIFFITHS

Chapter 4

While the era was busy producing new appliances, one item had more impact during this time than any other. Radio sales exploded during the decade. Radio's first commercial broadcast was the Harding-Cox presidential election in 1920. Although few people heard the broadcast, because there were few radios at the time, the magic of sound traveling through the air caught fire, and soon the demand for receivers was such that manufacturers could not keep up. The device changed American culture. Radio shows were developed and became sources of information and entertainment. Listeners followed westerns, soap operas, comedies, detective series, musicians, and religious sermons. Families gathered around the radio to laugh, cry, and listen to what was going on in the world outside their communities.

When I was a small girl, there was no television and there were very few radios. There was no electricity out in the country, so if you had a radio, it was used with batteries.

We also had a big Victrola, which you had to wind up to play each record. There was a crank on the side you had to wind before it would play. My brothers and I thought it was wonderful. We had a big collie dog called Rover, and when we played a certain record, he would howl. So in the summer you can imagine what we did. We would play it over and over, and Rover would stand on the front porch and howl until Mom would make us stop playing the record. Mom liked to hear her Billy Sunday records. Billy Sunday was a well-known preacher like Billy Graham was later.

On Sunday morning, Dad would play "Lazy Mary, Will You Get Up" so Mary would get out of bed. That would tickle us children.

My aunt Hattie and uncle Eli Treadway lived about a mile down the road from us, and they purchased a radio with batteries. The whole neighborhood was really glad about that, because now we could go hear the *Grand Ole Opry*, a show that played on Saturday night from Nashville. This was just about the time it started. It had Roy Acuff, Minnie Pearl, Uncle Dave Macon, and several more who were young and just starting their careers. Uncle Eli was short and fat, and had a sense of humor. Aunt Hattie was part Indian. We could hardly wait until Saturday night. Mom and Dad didn't go, so it was Mary, Raymond, Pete, and me. We had to take our Saturday night baths, because Sunday morning we went to Sunday school, and we would get home too late to take it and would be too tired.

We usually left about seven o'clock and had to walk the mile, as Mary didn't drive after dark and the roads were muddy. We had to wear overshoes most of the time and take a lantern. The boys used to fuss about which one would carry the lantern.

When we got to my uncle and aunt's home, several people would have arrived already. My aunt would have benches and chairs all around the living room and kitchen. She would have big pans of popped corn and popcorn balls. The adults had coffee, but I think the children had water.

Everyone had to sit down and be still once the radio show started. The children didn't play or make noise. The adults were real still and quiet. It was like going to a concert; you listened, applauded, and laughed when it was funny. Everyone stayed until midnight, and it was wonderful. I still like country music, and I think it was from listening to the *Grand Ole Opry* from those days as a child.

The walk going home seemed a lot longer than going because I was so tired, and I was so happy to get home and into a nice warm bed. When it was really cold outside, we used to heat the old irons and wrap them in a blanket and put them to our feet in the bed for warmth.

Uncle Eli and Aunt Hattie saved their battery for the radio so they could have it for Saturday nights. Once in a while through the week there was something special on, and they would telephone us to come and hear it. We had one of those telephones that hung on the wall that was on a party line service. Our ring was four rings.

We really enjoyed Uncle Eli and Aunt Hattie's radio, and so did plenty of other people. We didn't get our first radio until I was twelve years old, and it was a battery-operated one as well. We had to save it for evenings when everyone was in the house, but it was enjoyed very much.

Chapter 5

Iva Mae loved talking about family and spent several years researching the Treadway and Sissel families. She found the Treadway family line back to Edmund, who was born in Ireland about 1798 when the name was spelled Tredway. On the Sissel side, her research took her back to John Sissel, who was an early settler in Maryland and listed in her notes as "transported" in 1665. Iva Mae's notes weren't entirely clear, but the reference is likely associated with the Province of

Maryland's customs during these years, when people who "transported" themselves—or paid for their own transportation when they immigrated—were listed in the records books as such.

Iva Mae was happiest with her family around her, but only if she was the center of attention. She was a giving person, but she also wanted attention and in most cases demanded it. Her desire to be the center of any conversation reflected her need to feel wanted and loved. Throughout her life her mantra was "They like me." It was always important for Iva Mae to believe people liked her. Whenever she met someone new, whether she believed they were going to be significant to her or they were just having a passing conversation, she would say later, "They liked me." As a child she got attention with temper tantrums. As she grew older, she got noticed in different ways—but she always got the attention she required. It was speculated that because Iva Mae did not get the attention she needed as a child, she spent most of her life looking for positive reinforcement.

Being with her family and loved ones was important to her throughout her life, starting when she was a child and her oldest siblings would come to visit. Her oldest brother, Emmett, was married and lived in Parsons, Kansas, as did her sister Lula, who, with her husband, Roy, had started her family of four boys. Lula and Roy's oldest son, Dale, was only about three years younger than Iva Mae.

> When I was five years old, a disaster happened: our house burned!
>
> It was the last day of April and really cool and damp. School was to be out the next day, and it was tradition to

have a last-day dinner, which everyone around attended. Lula and Dale had come down on the train and were at our house to go with us. Dale was born at our house, and I thought he was so cute. When he was born, I told everyone he was my baby and I was going to keep him.

Dale was three years old and had been cranky, and Lula kept telling him she was going to take him upstairs and put him to bed. That evening Mary built a huge fire in the old cookstove to bake corn bread for supper. We always had corn bread and milk for supper. She was trying to entertain Dale that evening, so she would say she was baking corn dodger, and Dale would say, "No, it's corn bread." They argued all during the evening until after we ate, and he was still cranky, so Lula decided to put him to bed.

They put my and Dale's nightclothes on, and Lula carried Dale up the stairs. When she opened the door, the whole upstairs was full of smoke, so she shut the door and yelled, "The house is on fire!" Mom ran to the bedroom downstairs to see if the incubators were on fire. She had two incubators in the bedroom. They ran on kerosene, and you put eggs in them, and each day you would turn the eggs in the morning and in the evening. Sometimes Mom let me help her turn the eggs. When they hatched, you had baby chickens. Then when the chickens were grown, you had laying hens and roosters for food or to sell. But the incubators were not the cause of the fire.

Mary ran to the phone and cranked the handle to ring it several times. That was a general ring, and everyone listened. She told them the house was on fire. She grabbed up the big sewing machine and carried it out by herself, which in itself was amazing, as she was ill with tuberculosis and couldn't lift anything. She complained about it in later years, because the machine wasn't very good.

Lula took Dale and me to the car and wrapped a blanket around us, and we were supposed to stay there while everyone worked.

Soon the yard was full of cars and people. There were a lot of men and boys loafing at the garage in Labette, only a mile away from our home. As the people arrived, they started carrying out our stuff. There was no fire department. The upstairs was too far gone, so all our toys and other things that belonged to me and my brothers were gone. It was disappointing, since Santa Claus had been good to us that year. I had got a beautiful dark-haired doll for Christmas, but it was upstairs. All our family pictures, Mary's clothes, and her "hope chest" holding all the things she had made for when she got married were destroyed. She had tatted a lace bedspread, which went up in smoke.

The house was old but sturdy. It was called the Conner Place and made out of walnut lumber. There were two rooms upstairs for me, Mary, Raymond, and Pete. We had feather beds for mattresses. The house had an open staircase with a banister we used to slide down, like all children. The downstairs had a kitchen, pantry, dining room, parlor, and bedroom. The place had an old cellar under the house and concrete porches on the front and back.

The men were carrying things out as fast as they could. The house was full of prepared food, because the next day was the last day of school. When school ended, the people in the area would gather on the last day at the town hall and bring a basket of food, and the children would put on a program for the families. Mom had prepared a chicken for chicken and noodles, baked one of her huge cakes, and had several pies. The men carried the food out of the house and set it on the ground because there was nowhere else to put it.

Mom would buy PJ Soap by the dollars' worth, and you got a lot of soap for that amount of money. The men seemed to have fun throwing the soap out the doors of the burning house, but I'm sure it was the tension of getting it done as fast as possible. Pete and I used to have fun with the soap, playing with the boxes. We would build roads with them and use the old cast irons that you heated on the stove to iron clothes as our cars.

The incubators were then carried outdoors and left out all night. Mom said the eggs wouldn't hatch after that, but the next morning everything was put into the cellar, and believe it or not they did hatch—and even better than usual.

Almost everything in the downstairs was saved with the help of the men who came to empty the house. The upstairs was a different story, and unfortunately all was lost.

Roy, Lula's husband, was in Parsons about ten miles away. He had been playing cards at the post office, where he was a mail carrier. On the way to the farm, around midnight, he saw a big fire and said to a friend, "Wonder what is burning?" never dreaming his wife and son were there at the fire.

Finally it died down and we all went to Uncle Eli and Aunt Hattie's to stay the night. My parents would make plans the next day for what we would do and where we would live. Everyone was grateful that Dale had not been put to bed early.

Chapter 6

Iva Mae's recollections of those years continued: Living on a working farm is all consuming, and after the house burned, we had to find a way to stay. The animals on the farm needed attention. There were chickens to be fed, eggs to be collected, horses to be cared for, and cows that needed to be milked morning and evening. So my folks decided to fix up two granaries and the shed for us to live in while the house was being rebuilt. The shed was where we kept the car.

Our shed was transformed into a home. It became our living room, with the dining table and chairs so we could eat our meals. My folks put a bed and dresser in the shed as well. One of the granaries became the kitchen and we put the cookstove in there, so they fixed a place for the chimney to the stove. The other granary became a bedroom. We also had the telephone out there, which I thought was smart.

It was an exciting time for me because friends gave Mary a party that we called a "shower" for new clothes since hers had been all burned. We also were "showered" with quilts, blankets, and sheets since most of our bedding had been upstairs in the fire.

It was the last of April when the house burned, and we didn't get in the new house until July of that year. It was not always easy living in a barn. We had flies, and at our meals we constantly had to shoo them away, hoping they didn't fly into our mouth while we were eating. We could also hear the cows and horses since they were so close. Then there were rats and mice, which always sent chills down my spine because I was terrified that one would get on my bed.

I remember one night before we moved into the barn, when Mary and I stayed all night with Alma O'Farnell. Her family ran a store and had lots of candy, which we didn't get very often. I was just only five years old and I wanted a candy bar so bad, I could taste it, so I took one. Well, I got caught. Alma saw me take it, and she talked to me about it, too. She didn't tell Mary, but I never did take one again—and I still haven't forgotten about it to this day.

I could hardly wait to get into our new house. We watched them work every day building. In July they finished and we moved into our brand-new house. It was much different from our old house, which had been big and roomy. This was a small, five-room house with a screened-in porch. It had three bedrooms, one of which was hardly big enough for a bed. That room was for my brothers, Pete and Raymond. Mary and I had the front bedroom. Our room didn't have a closet, so Mary took sheets and made us one. Then we had a living room and kitchen. The house was very plain, with no built-in cabinets or bathrooms. But to me at six years old, who had just had a birthday, it was just fine. I lived there until I was twelve years old, and I still think of it as home.

ROBIN ANNE GRIFFITHS

Chapter 7

I va Mae's passions included family, holidays, food, and
later in life, her love of God. Many of her life stories were
about her family getting together, often during a holiday,
and the food that they prepared. Christmas was always an
important holiday for her family. For most of Iva Mae's life,
Christmas meant planning months in advance, whether it was
saving the money to buy gifts, putting the gifts on layaway, or
preparing the mass amount of cookies, candies, and other

treats to give or send to friends and relatives. Her food preparation was well known, and she enjoyed knowing that she was giving pleasure through her culinary efforts.

Perhaps life was enjoyed more because it was so precious, and family was important because they were your total support system. During Iva Mae's early years, before the discovery and widespread use of antibiotics and vaccinations, children who were exposed to multiple infections became ill and died. Strep throat, ear infections, and other serious infections such as pneumonia, whopping cough, and scarlet fever often were fatal or caused severe and lasting disabilities. The discovery of penicillin and the use of antibiotics began in the 1920s. But during the late 1800s and early 1900s, childhood diseases such as measles, mumps, smallpox, and chickenpox were deadly. And in the early 1900s, more than 50 percent of the children who died in America succumbed to a communicable disease.

I can remember Christmas being a very happy time. Dad would put a big tree in our parlor, and we would decorate it with popcorn and other homemade items. My sister Lula, with her husband and son, Roy and Dale, would come to stay. Also my brother Emmett, with his wife, Mabel, and their children, Marvin and Marjorie, would come home as well. It was a fun time as all us kids would sleep on the floor and giggle and talk.

Roy would show up on Christmas Eve as Santa Claus, and we would get so excited. Marjorie, who is six months older than me, always got the same things I did. Roy would make a lot of noise with Pete's old chains, and Pete would say, "Listen: Santa has my old chains."

Mom always prepared a huge dinner, because we were

one of those families that loved to eat. Mom was such a good cook. I weighed ten pounds when I was born and was big in size all my life. I also sucked my thumb until I was nine or ten years old. Then Raymond promised me a new dress if I would stop, so I did. I also had poison oak at the same time, so I was probably too busy scratching to suck my thumb anyway.

We really had a lot of fun when Marjorie, Marvin, and Dale came to the house. We would play in the big barn that had a haymow, which is where we had stored hay for the winter. Billy, who was older than Raymond, lived on the next farm. He teased me all the time, but I used to think he was just wonderful and I had a big crush on him. Billy called me Oney. Lois from the neighboring farm, who was six years older than me, also came to play. Although she and her people were odd, I still played with her. We spent time together in the summer too, going with the threshers. We would ride the grain wagons and our job was setting the table, keeping the drinks poured for the men, and taking water to them in the field. Dale and I really played well together, since we were so close in age. We would spend hours playing school or office. Marjorie and I were almost like sisters, too.

My birthday is July 3, so I always celebrated it the day before Independence Day. Mom let me have my birthday outdoors, so we would have a picnic. On the Fourth, we would have firecrackers and sparklers. Dad would get pop and watermelon, and we would make ice cream. Mom would fry chicken and prepare all the trimmings that would go with that meal. Everyone would come to our place for the day.

Also when I was three, my grandma Sissel died, so
Emmett, Mabel, Mom, Dad, Raymond, Pete, and I went
to the funeral in Arkansas. It rained terribly, and the roads
weren't good. We had to stop and put the side curtains on
the car. I can remember Uncle John carrying me around
and giving me gum. They had the funeral outdoors at the
house and then buried her at Rogers, Arkansas.

When I was small, every Sunday we would meet with all
the relatives for dinner, including Uncle Eli Treadway,
Aunt Hattie, and the Gerens, who were friends of the
family. They always let the men eat first, and then the
women, and the children last. We used to starve,
especially at the Gerens, because they were so slow and
particular. They always cleaned the stove before anyone
could eat. All of us children didn't like Mrs. Geren, so we
used to spend our time hiding from her, too.

When I was three years old, my mom, dad, Pete, and
Raymond and I went to Parsons on the train. We lived
ten miles from Parsons, so it was a trip to visit the home
of my brother Emmett. That night we went to see a
"talkie" movie show. That was a first, and I remember
that night I got really sick. My folks took me to the doctor
and I had scarlet fever. I was very sick and almost died. I
can remember no one could come to the house. Because I
was so contagious, Dad would go get the groceries and
they would set items outside for him to pick up. They
would call the order in on our phone, which was the kind
that hung on the wall. They fumigated our house, and we
all had to go to the barn when it was done.

Chapter 8

Raymond and Pete were Iva Mae's playmates for the most part in her younger years since they were still on the farm and closest to her age. Like most older children with a younger sibling, they did not welcome the idea that she wanted to do everything and go everywhere with them. As the story goes, Raymond teased Iva Mae unmercifully by putting cats or small chickens down her back, which made her not want to be around cats or other small, furry animals. For the rest of her life she did not like small animals or cats and preferred not to be around them. She tolerated dogs and later in life would laugh at how her children's dogs gave her so much unwanted attention. But even with the teasing, she and Raymond had a bond, and they spent time together over the years until his death in his eighties.

Raymond and Pete were only two years apart and looked alike as children. They had the same bowl-cut hair, and they often were dressed alike in their overalls and white shirts. Raymond was taller and thinner in the face, and Pete was a bit stockier. Both boys, as well as others in the family, had the same prominent chin—sort of a cross between round and square. As with most siblings, Iva Mae's brothers were supposed to look after her when they went to school or were playing around the farm. They teased her until she cried. Raymond was fast and smart, and if they were in trouble, he would run off and hide until their mother's temper cooled off.

> My two brothers Raymond and Pete, along with a neighbor boy, Billy, use to camp out in the yard, in the orchard, or down by the barn that ran near the road. I always wanted to go with them. In fact, I wanted to do everything they did, but you know boys just don't like little sisters tagging after them.

> So I would throw a temper tantrum, as usual, because that was the only way I got to do anything. My mom didn't feel good after I was born, so usually she would give in just to shut me up, and tell the boys I could go with them.

> Then the fun would start, because if I was going to go, I had to work and run errands. First I had to get wood to

cook our supper and poles to build our tent. We looked everywhere for old canvas and feed sacks, and sometimes Mom would give us an old quilt. We would put the canvas and sacks over the poles to make our tent. Then we had the quilt to put on the ground. We would work so hard that the sweat would be running off our faces.

Billy, the neighbor boy, was about seven years older than me, and I thought he was wonderful. I really had a crush on him. He called me Oney, because I was always starting all my sentences with *Only*. Fifty years later, I saw Billy again at my brother Pete's funeral. We knew each other immediately, and he still called me Oney.

When we got the tent up, we then had to build the fire and start our supper. The boys built the fire while I went to get the grub and skillet to cook the potatoes and bacon. It was an old, black iron skillet that I probably wouldn't use now, but Mom wasn't going to give us one of her good ones. We didn't care—we thought it was perfect.

I had to peel and slice the potatoes, which took forever. My knife was probably dull, because I am sure they wouldn't give a six- or seven-year-old a very sharp knife. We always had bacon, fried potatoes, and pork and beans, along with sugar cookies for dessert. Mom baked a batch of sugar cookies every week, so our cookie jar was never empty. We always thought the food we cooked was wonderful, even with ashes in it and flies swarming around it.

Carla, a little girl across the road from us, was younger than me and a real pest. Every time she came to our house, she wanted something to eat, but she didn't want a cracker or bread and jelly. She wanted something good like cake or pie. Mary and my mom hated to see Carla coming. Well, one evening Carla came out where we were camping and wouldn't go home. We were almost ready to eat and we didn't want to eat in front of her—but we didn't want to feed her, either. The boys tried every way to get Carla to go home, but no way would she go.

So we started acting like her mom and dad were calling her to come home. We would turn our backs and yell, "Carla, Carla, come home." Then we would turn back around and say, "Carla, your mom and dad are calling you to come home." At last her parents came and told her she had to go home. We were so glad, because then we could eat our supper.

Boy, did we eat! And when we were stuffed, you can guess who had to do the dishes. Me! I had to get some water from the well and wash the dishes while the boys tended the fire and got ready for night. By this time it was dark. The flies were gone, but you could see the lightning bugs coming out.

Mom would make me come to the house to sleep because I couldn't sleep with the boys. By this time I was so tired and sleepy that I was ready for my bath in the backyard and then bed. That was enough camping until the next time they went, but then I would be ready to go again, even if they made me do the work.

Chapter 9

I t is hard to imagine farm life during the late 1920s and early 1930s. Most of their food was grown or raised on the property. Gardens were a staple for meals, and canning food to have it in winter was a necessity. Iva Mae commented more than once that her family didn't seem to feel the Depression on the farm like people in the cities and towns did. She said they always had food on the table and she didn't feel like they suffered from a lack of anything. The times were different and expectations for material things were low, so having food on the table and a treat now and then was enough.

When I was growing up on the farm, we waited patiently until the cold frost days set in, usually in November or early December. We couldn't butcher until it got really cold, but we liked to get that done before Thanksgiving or at least Christmas.

Usually they shut the hogs up and fed them lots of corn before they were butchered, so they would be fat. Finally the big day would arrive, with Mom and Dad getting up at least by five in the morning. Dad was one of those parents who made all the children get up early. We had to dress, come downstairs, and wash our faces in cold water. If we did this, according to Dad, we would never have wrinkles. Even if we had friends over for company, they had to wash their faces in cold water. Pete and I didn't mind getting up, and we had to have our coffee. He and I drank coffee from the time we were born. But Raymond never wanted to get up, and Dad would threaten to get the razor strap if he didn't. By the time we got our clothes on, there was a warm fire built in both woodstoves and breakfast on the table.

For butchering you had to have a lot of boiling water, so they built big fires outdoors and filled big black kettles with water to heat. It had to be boiling so you could get a good scald. The neighboring men always came to help butcher, and then Dad would go help them in return.

They had a big barrel they would put the scalding water in, and it usually sat on a platform. Our platform was a sled and Dad would take us to school on it when it snowed, which was always fun. We would stop along the road to pick up the neighbor children on our way.

While the water was being put in the big barrel, someone who was good at killing hogs was getting ready for the first hog. They usually shot it with a .22 gun, but sometimes someone would knock it in the head with a hammer. They had to stick the hog as soon as they killed him so the blood would drain. If the hog didn't bleed out, the meat wouldn't be good. The hog was then doused in the barrel of hot water, up and down until the hair began to slip off. Afterward the hog was placed on a table or platform and the remaining hair was scraped off. If you didn't get a good scald, it was hard to get the hair to slip off. The head always had to be cleaned; that was a hard job that nobody wanted to do. They used the brains and also made mincemeat and souse out of the head.

After they cleaned the hog, they would dip it in cold water and hang it by the feet. We had a big hay barn with a pulley, so that is where we hung our pigs. Then one of the men with a sharp knife would cut the hog open and take out the entrails. They had to make sure they didn't cut the gall bladder, because that would spoil the liver and part of the meat.

Usually all us children would be standing with a pan so we could take the liver to the house so the women could cook it for dinner for the men. They always had gravy and hot biscuits to go with the liver.

When the men's work ended, the women had to start cutting the fat off the entrails and getting everything ready to make lard. They usually built a big fire outdoors and put a black kettle on the fire full of the fat off the hog. Someone had to stay with the kettle and stir it all the time with a big stick, because you couldn't let it catch on fire. Once it was done, the fat was skimmed off the surface of the mixture. That was lard, our shortening or Crisco of the time.

The hog was left to hang until cool, and the next day it was cut into hams, shoulders, and tenderloin. The side meat that came off the ham, shoulders, and tenderloin was ground up into sausage. My mom and Mary then made sausage patties out of it and canned it into quart jars.

The hams, shoulders, and side meat were salted and later hung in the old smokehouse for long hours of hickory smoking. That sure was some good eating. We used to pickle the feet, and I remember having that for supper. The house used to be greasy until they got all the meat worked up. The next morning after butchering, we would climb out of bed smelling cooked tenderloin with biscuits and gravy—and thinking that butchering time wouldn't be for another year.

Chapter 10

Throughout her life, Iva Mae was always ready to have a meal outdoors, whether it was a picnic by a stream, a barbecue at the park, or a reunion at a family member's home. She so enjoyed the family being together and having a good meal with her loved ones, and looked forward to such events with excitement. Her love of food and family was the center of her life, besides her love of God in her later years.

Raymond's daughter, Sally, became good friends and close to Iva Mae later in life. Sally shared her favorite story about Iva Mae: "Occasionally I make potato salad, a job that I don't particularly enjoy so it doesn't happen often, maybe once or twice in the summer." Well, Iva Mae and Aunt Lula evidently had a good time giggling together about other women's talents or lack thereof in the potato-salad-making department, because Sally said that Aunt Lula, after sampling some at a reunion or gathering, would whisper to Iva Mae, "I'm going to go home and make some *good* potato salad!" The ability to make good potato salad became a family joke.

> Lula was my sister and Roy my brother-in-law but more like a brother to me. My life would have been empty without them when I was young. I was one year old when they got married and moved to Kansas City. Everyone loved to ask me where they lived because I couldn't pronounce *city*. They didn't live up there very long before they moved back to Labette. I claimed their son Dale as my baby, and we were always close and kept in touch throughout our lives.

> I remember visiting them at Labette. I thought Lula was the best cook, and her eggs and peas were especially wonderful. I didn't know she got eggs from my mom. Her peas were canned, and my mom canned peas that came from our garden.

> Lula and Roy soon moved to Parsons, where Roy became a mail carrier. Labette was just ten miles from Parsons, and there was a train you could ride to get there.

> Roy loved to fish and we lived on a creek, so they would come every weekend. Roy and Lula had several friends,

and in the summer they all came to the farm and camped out, so of course Raymond, Pete, and I were with them. They would build fires, and we would get straw and put blankets on the straw to sleep. Roy would bake beans in the ground. One time he burnt his pants up and had to borrow a pair from Dad.

There wasn't anyone quite like Roy, although he had a temper. One time we were down on the creek and Roy had a flat tire. When the jack wouldn't work, he threw it in the creek—and then made Pete and Raymond walk into the creek to retrieve it for him.

Roy, Lula, and I would play a card game called canasta, which is similar to rummy. Roy didn't like to lose, so one night when Lula and I were winning, he said we were going to keep playing until he won. We finally stopped at three in the morning, with me and Lula still winning.

Roy was most known for pretending he was asleep on the couch. He would just snore, but Lula and I knew he wasn't asleep. We would talk about how cute he was and what beautiful curly hair he had, and he would begin to grin. Roy loved fishing better than anything. One time he went fishing down at Labette Creek bridge, but when he jumped out of the car, he didn't turn his car off. Roy fished all afternoon, and when he got back to the car, the battery was dead.

He used to let his son Dale and me walk with him on his mail route. We loved to do this because Roy was friends with everyone and their dogs, too. Roy was so much fun playing with us when we were kids. He would play all kinds of games with us, like putting a sheet over his head and scaring us. He would tease me and shake my chin so I couldn't talk, and he was always singing to us. When several of us kids stayed all night at Roy and Lula's home, he would tie our clothes all together as a prank.

My sister Lula was really something special. She loved her family. She never said anything bad about anyone, and she didn't want anyone else to, either.

Roy and Lula had a small house—and I mean small—but she never cared how often we went over or how long we stayed. She would cook all our favorite meals and do our washing and ironing. She would wait on us and take care of our needs. She was always the first one to the car when somebody drove up, and when they left, she gave them a present and walked them to the car.

Lula supplied me with spending money when I was in high school, and she bought me cloth for dresses and Mary would make them. When I was up there visiting them, we went on picnics and to fairs and movies. We would go to a park or Lake McKinley and cook breakfast. We used to cook everything, even pancakes or doughnuts, on those trips.

When a fair or circus came to Parsons, Roy would come and get Raymond, Pete, and me to go with them. Later when I started teaching, he took me to Oak Valley and Howard—a hundred miles away—to apply for schools. When I came home on weekends, he would take me back.

After I had my son, Denny, I wasn't well, and we lived a hundred miles from the hospitals in either Wichita or Parsons. So I would go and stay with Lula and Roy. Much later, when I was married to Bob and Robin was born, we were both out of a job. So once again, I stayed with Roy and Lula. Lula was with me when I had all of my children. I will never forget them, and I have a special place in my heart for their sons, Dale, Darrell, Duane, and Dean.

Lula was not an especially attractive woman, but her heart showed through so much, you couldn't help but smile and love her. She was always smiling, and Roy loved to tease, and they seemed to have a happy life together. Roy passed away in 1960 at sixty-five, and Lula in 1970 at sixty-eight. The day that Lula passed away, Robin was called out of class at junior high school and told her mother was coming to pick her up. Robin could see her mother was very upset, and Iva Mae said that her sister Lula had passed away.

Iva Mae's stories about her sister and Roy did not adequately convey the warmth of this family, who lived in a very small house, but even now, Robin can remember the joy this couple had and shared. Occasionally Robin would be compared to Lula and feel proud that she had some of her qualities. Family events at their home were special. Children always had plenty of toys to play with during the visit. Lula collected rocks of different shapes and colors from her various travels and would happily show anyone her collection with the story attached. Everyone would have more than enough food, and all enjoyed each other's company. All who visited their home could feel that something was special about this woman and her giving and loving spirit.

ROBIN ANNE GRIFFITHS

Chapter 11

During the mid-1930s, Kansas had three big challenges—the Depression, despair, and dust storms. Many people worked for the national Works Progress Administration (WPA), which employed millions to build public works projects such as parks, schools, and roads. Parsons was and still is the most populous city in the county. The town of Labette was founded in 1870, and during the time Iva Mae was growing up, the Missouri-Kansas-Texas Railroad, which came to be known as "the Katy," was a vital part of the community.

As Iva Mae was moving into her teenage years, her mother's health continued to decline. Her father was focused on the farm, and Iva Mae's relationship with him and her mother was distant, mainly because of the circumstances. She looked to her sisters for guidance and support. Although her sisters did not live on the farm and were not involved in Iva Mae's daily life, she looked to them more as motherly figures.

It's quite possible Iva Mae missed having a strong bond with her mother, perhaps because she was the youngest in her family and her mother became so ill after she was born. She appeared to need attention more than most people and had narcissistic tendencies, requiring positive reinforcement from others. Even as a child she would have a temper tantrum or center the conversation on herself to get the attention she required. From her earliest years Iva Mae needed and demanded to be noticed. Although she would do almost anything for anyone, her relationships with family members were always more about herself and how they affected her. She was not known to be very emotional other than when it was about her feelings or something that was upsetting her directly. Times were different for a young child growing up during her era. Prospects and life expectancy were precious, and people had to be strong to survive.

Iva Mae's cousin Dean, Lula and Roy's youngest son, had memories of those early years:

> I was born in the little house on Chess Street in Parsons, Kansas, in 1936. I was the fifth son born to Roy and Lula Mullen. I had three older brothers who survived and two

brothers who died as infants. We lived in the small house
until I was in the first or second grade. At that time, Iva
Mae was living with her family at the house in Labette
City, about eight or nine miles southeast of Parsons.
During this time, either 1938 or 1939, our grandmother,
Iva Mae's mother, was very sick and bedfast. I am sure it
was difficult for Iva Mae, who was still living at home
with her brother Pete. Those were not good times.

I remember at age three going to their house each
Saturday with groceries, and Iva Mae and my mother
doing all the laundry. They would also do all the cooking
and nursing for my grandmother. My memory of that
time is scant, but I can remember my grandmother being
ill and confined to a bed in the corner of the kitchen,
close to the heat of the stove. I believe she had female
cancer, and she always smelled very strong. She died
shortly after this time.

Her mother's illness colored many of Iva Mae's memories
of her:

Although my mother was a generous person, she had
strict beliefs. She would do as much for the neighbors as
she could and give them anything she had to give. My
sisters said I didn't know her very well. She was thirty-
eight when I was born, and she was always sick
afterwards. I knew her to be very religious, but my sisters
said she used to be a lot of fun. They used to do things
like go swimming after working in the garden. My mom
was a worker. She did all the things a farm woman would
do. She would help milk the cows, raise a big garden, help
in the fields, and can the food for future use. She was also

a wonderful cook.

When I was nine years old, she took sick and had to have an operation. The day she was operated on, the family all gathered at the hospital in Oswego, Kansas. At that time, when you were having surgery, the doctors gave you ether as an anesthesia. When she was waking up after the surgery, she screamed. Of course, we could hear her. I was scared to death.

My two aunts came from Missouri, along with my two sisters and brother, so all the family was there at the hospital. Raymond, Pete, and I didn't go to school that day. When she came home, she got better till I was about twelve or thirteen years old. Then she started vomiting and she had diarrhea. My sister Mary had married, so I had to do a lot of housework since my mom was unable to do much. Some days she could be up, but some days she couldn't get out of bed. Lula began to come down at the end of the week and stay to do our washing, and then she'd return to her home on Sunday. I missed a lot of school because someone had to stay with my mom. I hated to carry her chamber pot, and would raise a fuss about it, as would any typical teenager.

When I was fifteen and school had been out, she was getting worse. I am sure she had some kind of cancer. She had dropped from around two hundred to eighty pounds. One rainy day in June, my dad had gone to work on the WPA. Pete and Raymond were then working at the Kraft Cheese factory.

That day Raymond's car would not start, and he wanted me to come out and drive it while he pushed it to get it started. He knew I didn't know how to drive. Well, I drove it right into the ditch. We then got into a big fight out in the street before he left for work. Later that afternoon, Mom woke up and told me she had a dream. She wanted me to go up to the store and call Lula. She wanted Lula and Emmett to come down home that evening.

Dad arrived first, then Lula and Roy, Emmett and Mabel, and finally Pete. They were all around her bed as she was laughing and telling them about the fight that Raymond and I had had that morning over the car incident in the street. Someone said, "Here's Raymond." And at that moment, my mother gave a gasp and died laughing. That made such a big impression on me, because I am sure she had a message from God telling her she was going to die. So she had me get the family together for her last goodbye.

Iva Mae Treadway
High School Graduation Announcement

Chapter 12

After the death of her mother, Iva Mae's life changed. She was only fifteen and had missed much of her junior year at school while staying home to care for her mother. She stayed with a friend while completing her senior year and graduated in 1939 at the age of sixteen. That year she went on a senior trip to New Orleans, which must have been sponsored by the school since Iva Mae had little money. She was able to go even though she had very few clothes for such a trip. Later in life she would laugh about how she washed out her belongings daily to have clean items to wear. That may have been the catalyst that sparked her interest in travel and discovering new places. She loved reading, and a family that lived near her growing up had an extensive home library to which Iva Mae was welcomed. That is where she learned to love Louisa May Alcott, Gene Stratton-Porter, Zane Grey, and various other authors. She was often caught staying up late reading her books or reading books for her brothers and doing their book reports for them.

Iva Mae's father moved in with Lula and Roy not long after his wife's death. Lula and Roy's son Dean recounted those years in some detail:

> After Grandmother died, our grandfather moved in with my family. I believe Iva Mae was in school and returned to our house each weekend. This was tough on my momma, as we didn't have any room and we were always short with money.
>
> Our house held all of us somewhere. Mom and Dad slept on a daybed in the kitchen, and Granddad had a small bed in the bedroom with the boys. Our house was small with only three rooms—a front room with a large coal stove; a small bedroom that held two full beds, a daybed, and a small closet; a tiny bathroom with a tub; and a small kitchen that held my parents' bed and an icy box. We had no hot water and an old dilapidated garage that we all were afraid to use.
>
> Each room had an electric bulb hanging from the ceiling. I can remember my mother always wishing to have a lamp, but I can't remember her ever getting one. We did

have a radio, and we listened each night until around eight thirty. Then we all went to bed at the same time, and we all got up at six in the morning to start the day.

Our grandfather was becoming belligerent and starting to wander off, and it seemed I was always sent to try and find him. I was four at the time, and I would go as many as six blocks away to look for him and hold his hand in my fist to lead him back home.

Shortly before the war, in the spring of 1941, my uncle Raymond, Iva Mae's brother, returned from Hawaii and left the army. He rented a house right across from the rear of our house and moved my grandfather in with him. I believe Iva Mae was in school during this time. Uncle Raymond found a job with the Frisco Railroad, and I started kindergarten that September of 1941. Everything started to change about this time.

My mom and dad worried about Iva Mae not having the clothes she needed to start work. My father was off work at the time with heart issues, and Momma went to work at the laundry. She worked Monday through Friday, plus Saturday until noon. She was paid cash in a little manila envelope, with her hours and withholdings on the outside and her pay inside. She was getting a little over thirteen dollars per week at the time. Dad and Momma decided that they could afford to spend up to fifteen dollars on Iva Mae so she could get some clothes. It sounded like a lot at the time.

Then Sunday morning, December 7, Japan bombed Pearl Harbor and life changed for us all. Most young men at the time, including Iva Mae's brothers Pete and Raymond, rapidly became soldiers or sailors and were quickly sent to where they were most needed. Construction on the Kansas Army Ordnance Plant, three miles east of Parsons, began in 1941, and by November of 1942 nearly eleven thousand employees worked there. Everyone had jobs and made three to four times what they were earning before the war. There were lots of marriages followed by just a night or two in bed, and then the husbands were gone to war and the wives were all working and waiting for their men to come home. Women no longer stayed at home. They were farming, railroading, delivering the mail, and filling all the jobs vacated by the men who were gone.

Since so many parents were working long hours, they were no longer able to keep track of their children, who were often turned loose. We were on our own, free until the first parent returned from work. By this time, Iva Mae was seventeen or eighteen years old and teaching in a country school. She was not able to come home often, because gas was rationed and hard to come by. I remember her coming home by train just after the war started and before Grandpa died, which was the day after Christmas. I was always excited when she came home on the train. The Parsons Katy Depot was always busy during the war, with eighteen scheduled passenger trains daily in and out of Parsons going north and south. Later on they added on the prisoner of war trains going through, and they always fed the prisoners while in Parsons.

Chapter 13

One-room schools were commonplace in rural Kansas during the first half of the twentieth century. The teachers taught basic reading, writing, and arithmetic to all the boys and girls. The schools had limited supplies, usually consisting of a blackboard, student desks, a teacher's desk, maps, and sometimes a globe or perhaps a piano. A big old potbellied stove in the middle of the room provided warmth, water came from an outside pump, and an outhouse stood within a short distance of the school. It was the teacher's responsibility to clean the floors, fire up the stove, and shovel a path through the snow to the outhouse. For farm families, local schools were a necessity for educating their children, because transportation to the cities was neither convenient nor practical.

My mother died during my junior year of high school, so I stayed in a room during my senior year at Altamont, Kansas. I had a roommate, Catherine, who became a lifelong friend. Neither of us had any clothes or money at the time. We both took the Normal Training Course, which allowed us to teach with only a high school diploma if we passed the two-day exam at the end of the year. I was only sixteen years old when I took the exam, but I passed.

No schools in Labette County needed teachers, but about a hundred miles away in Elk County, there were vacancies. So I went over there and got a teaching position in a rural school out in the country, about two miles from Oak Valley, Kansas, and five miles from Longton. The school sat out on the prairie without a tree. A family that lived about a half mile from the school said I could board with them for eighteen dollars a month if I went home on weekends or twenty dollars if I stayed on weekends. I didn't have a car or know how to drive, so I stayed with them full time. My salary was sixty dollars a month.

On the first day of school, my legs were shaking. I was afraid I wouldn't remember to salute the flag, recite the Lord's Prayer, and sing "America, the Beautiful" every morning.

In my one-room schoolhouse, I built a fire in the coal stove when it was cold. The classroom had a water bucket with a dipper, and I took my lunch to school with me. At noon and during recess, I played with the children.

When my children arrived, there were seven of them. One girl was in first grade. Three children were in third grade, including one mentally retarded girl who was twelve years old and should have been in first grade. She had two brothers, a nine-year-old in fourth grade and a thirteen-year-old in sixth grade. Two girls were in seventh grade, although one of them was already fifteen years old.

So I started my first year of teaching in a school on a mud road—and I do mean mud. The mud came up over my boots. Many days in the winter when we had snow, the children did not show up for class. So I would build a fire and read or work on things, and then go home at about two o'clock in the afternoon.

One good thing about teaching in a one-room school was the box suppers, when everyone brought boxes of food or pies. The area families who attended the box suppers would put their best food in the boxes and then decorate the boxes, which also helped to keep the contents a secret. The boxes were auctioned off to the highest bidders, so the boys and men who were buying them would always try to find out in advance what was in each box. It was exciting to find out what was in those boxes. The school would put on a program, and everyone had a good time. The money we made on the boxes of food was used to buy something for the children to play with at the school or books for the classroom.

We always went out and cut down a Christmas tree and trimmed the school for the holiday, and then put on a program. Blanche, one of my sixteen-year-old students, could chord, so she played the piano for our singing. I am sure we weren't good quality, because I couldn't sing, but we had fun anyway. Remember, I was just seventeen years old myself.

When I went home to Parsons to visit, a family in the area would take me to Oak Valley. I would take a bus to Independence, Kansas, and then a trolley to Parsons. The trolley from Independence to Parsons would cost thirty cents for a thirty-mile ride. I stayed at South Oak Ridge for two years. But then I wanted more money, so I went to Starr School up around Piedmont, Kansas, for sixty-five dollars a month.

Starr School was at the edge of the Flint Hills, about sixty-eight miles from Wichita, Kansas, eight miles to Piedmont, and fifteen miles to Howard, Kansas. I found a place to board with a family about a mile and a half from the school. Helen, the wife, was a lousy housekeeper but a good cook. They had a small boy five years old, and when they wanted to go somewhere, they sent him to school with me.

This was a better school overall, but I still had to build fires and sweep, and the furnace was in the basement. It was out in the open fields with not one tree, but the road to school was gravel instead of mud, which was good for me since I had to walk to the school.

I had nine pupils until a new family moved into the district. The mother came and told me she was bringing some new students the next day. When I asked how many, she told me ten. She had fourteen children, so my class increased to nineteen pupils with at least one in every grade. I had four in the first grade and four in the eighth grade. I was really busy. It was hard to get all the lessons in, but I did get it done.

When I went home to Parsons, I rode the train from Piedmont to Cherryvale and then took the trolley to Parsons. On Thanksgiving I was going home on Wednesday night. The family I boarded with took me to the station. I turned out school early and got home to be ready to leave, but the family wasn't there. I waited and was really nervous. Finally they came, but it was late. When we got to Piedmont, the train was there, but we couldn't get across the track. I was determined to get on that train. I crawled under the train with my suitcase and broke my garter belt, and my hose came down around my ankle. I got on the train with my stockings around my shoes. I was so embarrassed when I got on and some boys were on the train that I knew. They had been to Wichita to sign up for the army. The war was beginning.

Me and the students at the Starr School put on programs, decorated for holidays, and played softball with other schools. I was always the pitcher for the team. I was nineteen years old, and this is where I met my husband, Em. He lived five miles from the school and had taught this school several years before.

I married Em just before the school year was over. We

went to Kansas City to his sister's home. I wasn't going to tell the school until the year was over, but Dr. Moon, a resident in town, took the paper and saw our marriage license notification. He and several others who knew us came and got me the night we got back from Kansas City, and had a shivaree. A shivaree was a celebration for newlyweds with a noisy mock-serenade to wish them well, involving the banging of saucepans, kettles, and other objects. The custom included friends coming to your home and you treating them with a party of candy, cigars, and other treats. Many times the couple would be dumped into a pond, or someone would put salt in their wedding bed, and there was often lots of noise from shooting guns. Me and Em's shivaree was tame compared to many. Someone took Em to Piedmont, where he got cigars and candy. We made coffee and had a good time. My schoolkids thought it was very funny. On the last day of school, I put on a program and they had a dinner and shivaree for me.

I was on my way to becoming a farm woman, raising chickens and a garden. I learned how to drive on a blue Chevy 1934 pickup truck. I drove in the pastures looking for cattle. So here a new life started for me with many new changes. My dad died that year on the day after Christmas, and the war had begun with Pearl Harbor.

Iva Mae was nineteen years old and needed a home. Em gave her a home and taught her how to cook, clean, take care of chickens and their eggs, drive a car and a tractor, and even make home brew. They had lots of company and threw beer parties. Over the years, Iva Mae told little snippets of her years with Em—all the company they had in their home and the parties they attended. One such story, involving a lot of drinking, had Iva Mae running down the main street of town wearing Em's boots and cowboy hat. Apparently he was chasing her and trying to lasso her with a rope. To this day, her children cannot picture this story as a reality. Not their mother! And yet they *can* believe she would be doing that in a heartbeat, since she was pretty daring in her own way.

South Oak Ridge School

Starr School

Chapter 14

Emerson Dennis Wyant, known by everyone as Em, was born in June 1893, so he was twenty-nine years older than Iva Mae. The Wyant family was from Ohio and came to Kansas by wagon in the late 1800s. Em was a cowboy, farmer, formerly a schoolteacher, and a member of the school board. He was a veteran of World War I, having served in the army in the south of France.

Iva Mae and Em were married in April 1941 in Kansas City. From looking at photos of Em, one could describe him as a good-looking young boy who grew into a tall, handsome, strong, and confident man. His son Dennis remembers him being pretty much bald but in his younger years having red hair and a light complexion. He wore a full-brimmed hat and had leathery skin, which would give him a two-toned look in summer: extremely white on top and red below. The wedding photo of Iva Mae and Em shows the vast age difference between them but also the happiness on Iva Mae's face. Her round face and large smile show her joy.

Iva Mae's nephew Dean remembers first meeting Em:

> The first time I saw Em, I was probably six or seven years old. He and Iva Mae had come to meet my family. At this time I had never heard a word of profanity in my home, and I actually thought my momma would die at first mention of it. Well, Em had never had a conversation that didn't start with, "Well, dammit to hell." But within a few minutes I could see that my parents liked him. I know that Momma was worried that Em was older and his drinking bothered her, but I know that she was fond of him. As far as I was concerned, he was the first cowboy I had ever known, and I never knew anyone who worked as he did. I loved him. He was great with me. He fanned me a few times when I needed it, but he was always good with me.

Iva Mae recalled her first years of married life:

> The spring and summer after I had got married I hadn't signed for a school because I was sick a lot. I was in the hospital three times at Eureka, Kansas. They thought I was pregnant but I wasn't. Finally, Jessie, Em's sister, came from Kansas City and got me. I entered a hospital

up there and they operated on me. I had tumors on my ovaries; my appendix was ready to burst, and I had a tumor on my adrenal gland. I was really sick with a special nurse for three days. Then Lula came and stayed with me a week. Em came till he had to go back to the farm. It was hay time, and we had cattle and horses.

Anyway, I was in the hospital four weeks and nearly died, but the Lord wasn't ready for me. But I bounced back and went home on the train to Parsons and stayed a few days, and then Em came after me. I wasn't home long before High Hill needed a teacher, so I started teaching again.

High Hill was located on the other side of Howard, Kansas, so I had to drive about sixteen miles. Some was mud roads with a hill. I stayed with two families. The first part of the school year I stayed with a family that let the fire go out at night. I would freeze. The last part I stayed with another family that had cats licking out the bowls on the tables. I was pregnant by then, and that didn't do anything for me. I would drive over Monday morning and then go home Wednesday night. Then I would come back Thursday morning and go home Friday night.

This school was about like the others, only older. I did get eighty dollars a month. I remember the Christmas program. I asked one of the board members to be Santa Claus and he was good, but he took his mask off when he got through, which disappointed the little children.

I taught till school was out but didn't take another school. Both schools close to me wanted me, but I was going to have Denny in October. Also I needed to go to summer school and the college was in Emporia, which was just too far away. So I settled down to be a farm wife and mom.

Iva Mae shared stories of her pregnancy, telling her children how she didn't do anything for exercise and gained a great amount of weight. It made for a very hard birth, she said, and it taught her a lesson, and with future children she watched how much weight she gained. Some of her inactivity could probably be attributed to the recovery from all her traumatic illnesses and surgeries. She told others more than once how they cut her open on one side to operate on her and then flipped her over to cut and operate on the other side. Later in life it was discovered that she had only one kidney, and it's believed that she lost the first one during this disturbing surgery. While pregnant with Denny, she was lazy, spending her days reading because she loved to read.

Em took care of most of the chores and was teaching her how to cook and take care of things, since she had had little training from her mother—although according to her nephew Dean, Iva Mae's cooking skills were the best:

> I don't know whether you are aware or not but Iva Mae baked the best devil's food chocolate cake. She liked to bake and at the time was coming to see us on weekends, and she would bake for us. She always baked a large cake for the family and we would eat it hot right out of the oven. Once, my brother Darrell got to mine before I knew it and ate a large piece of it. I remember just raising a fit until my mother paddled me and put me to bed to shut me up. I finally fell asleep, and when I woke up, Iva

Mae had baked me another for myself. Just one reason I loved her.

ROBIN ANNE GRIFFITHS

Chapter 15

It's amazing how little wars have affected Iva Mae's family in regard to loss. Iva's brother Emmett served in World War I and then came home, started his career, and raised his family. He lived for ninety-one years. Iva Mae's husband Em was also in World War I and served in the army in the south of France. He did see some combat, although he avoided exposure to mustard gas, but he received a back injury and some hearing damage. Both of Iva Mae's brothers served in

World War II. Pete saw heavy battle in Africa, and Raymond ended his career as an army major, having served in World War II and then later in Korea. Raymond passed away in 2005 and is buried in Arlington National Cemetery. More people died in World War II than in any other war in history; about 3 percent of the world's population of the 1940s era was killed. American casualties alone numbered more than four hundred thousand, a figure eclipsed only by the Civil War.

At the end of World War II a great many Americans lived in poverty. Many of the country's homes lacked electricity, running water, toilets, or central heating. But life was beginning to change for many, and prosperity from an economic boom was just beginning.

> Em and I lived on a farm in the Flint Hills located in Elk County, Kansas. It was a cold and windy place. There were no trees, and it sat out in the wide open spaces.

> We had a four-room house that was fairly new, but it wasn't modern, with a wood cookstove and a coal heating stove. Denny was two years old. This was the year the Second World War ended and everyone was coming home. They wrote to me that they were all meeting at our home to have Thanksgiving dinner.

> I was thrilled and we were so lucky. My two brothers Raymond and Pete, along with my two nephews Dale and Marvin, had all been in the war and came home alive. Pete had really been in the heavy part of it and came home with malaria fever, and he was terribly nervous, but he was all in one piece.

> I hadn't done a whole lot of cooking but was learning

with the help of my husband. He was a good cook. When we were first married, I would fix his breakfast and then he would fix mine. My breakfast would be the best.

There would be about thirty coming for the day and four staying for the weekend. It didn't seem to worry me too much, as I went to Howard the day before. Denny and I got all the groceries we needed and went out to a girlfriend's for lunch, which we really enjoyed. We went home about four that afternoon.

When my husband came in from doing chores and we put Denny to bed, then we started in by killing six hens and dressing them so I could bake them the next morning and make dressing. I made a big batch of noodles and put them out to dry. It was my mom's recipe, and I had good luck. I baked two cakes and made six pumpkin pies. Em made the piecrust while I was making the filling. He could make better piecrust than I could. About midnight we went to bed so we could get up early. The next morning Em got up early and built fires in the cookstove so I could bake the hens and make the dressing.

About ten o'clock they all came together. They drove from Parsons, Kansas, which was about a hundred miles. It was so good to see everyone and especially the boys.

The house was so small, the children all played in the bedroom. It was terribly cold that day and the wind was really howling. Our outhouse sat out by the barn and it was a long walk out there, and everyone would put off going out there as long as they could. There were a lot of jokes about going out to the bathroom.

Em was a bachelor and lived by himself until he married me, so he had the outhouse out by the barn so it was handy for him. He also had breeding horses. He had a Morgan stallion and a jack. The jack would bray every time someone would go to the outhouse.

We just had a small table, but we got everything on it for dinner plus using the cabinet and card table. Everyone was standing everywhere and children were setting all over the floor, but we had a good dinner.

It turned out wonderful and everyone went home saying, "Iva Mae cooked just like Mom." My mom died when I was fifteen and Em really had taught me to cook and clean and cut up a chicken.

It was really a blessing to have all the family together after being so worried about the war. All the rations that had gone on for so long were finally over, gas, shoes, and sugar and for some people, cigarettes and nylons.

As they were driving out of the driveway, I said, "Thank you all for getting home safe and sound." It had been a wonderful day.

Chapter 16

D ennis (Denny) Ray Wyant was born in October 1943 in Parsons, Kansas. According to Iva Mae's story, she went into labor, and she and Em took off for her sister Lula's home, where Denny Ray was born. His mother described him as a lively boy.

> Denny was one jump ahead and had an answer for everyone. One time when he was four years old and we lived north of Oak Valley, Kansas, on a farm, there was an oats field across the road from our

home. It was just about as tall as Denny. One of the neighbor women that lived close to us had come to get her mail and was coming by our house. She yelled, "What are you doing out there, Denny?" Denny replied, real serious, "Just looking for piss ants."

Em thought Denny was wonderful and took him everywhere. He used to go to parties with his parents. Em also taught Denny at an early age about ranching and farming. Iva Mae told her children that Em would let Denny do anything and he was his dad's boy. Denny has described his former teacher parents as being educational and giving valuable life lessons. Their interest in education was passed on to him. When an old schoolhouse was being torn down, they purchased many of the books, and Iva Mae read them all to Denny more than once. Iva Mae taught math and reading skills, and Em taught Denny geography.

Iva Mae was in her twenties when Denny was born. Their ranch had a four-room house and a large barn. Their life was much like many of their neighbors'. She and Em had their own responsibilities. Iva Mae did the cooking and cleaning but also planned for the butchering of pork, beef, and chicken for the winter. She also decided what to plant in the garden and then harvest for canning or storing in the cellar so they would have vegetables, fruits, jellies, jams, and pickles in winter. Other chores included raising chickens and gathering their eggs.

On the Wyant farm in the 1940s, taking care of everyday chores was a process. They did not have electricity at the time. Laundry or "washing" was done outside in a big black kettle where the water was heated over a fire. The clothes were washed, rinsed, and wrung through a wringer, then hung on a clothesline to dry. Having dairy cows, Iva and Em could be gone from home only a few hours, as the cows would need to be milked every morning at five and every evening at five. The milk was put in ten-gallon milk cans and kept cool in the horse and cow watering trough until a truck would stop by to pick it up to have it processed. During the wheat harvest time, both Em and Iva Mae would be in the fields from sunup to sundown. Em drove the combine to collect the wheat and empty it into the pickup truck bed, and Iva Mae drove it into the storage bins by the railroad. During hay season, Iva Mae drove the pickup while Em loaded the bales.

Since 1939 and *The Wizard of Oz*, Kansas has been known as Tornado Alley. Iva Mae was always a worrier, but storms intensified her fears throughout her life. Most Kansas farms had a root cellar, which served two purposes. A cellar was an important part of farm life because it held the harvest of potatoes, onions, and carrots, plus the canned fruit and vegetables and other food stored for the winter months when the farm was not producing. The structure was built underground, for the most part, and usually close to the farmhouse. When storms threatened, it served as a shelter where the family would run for protection.

There was such a cellar on Mary's—Iva Mae's sister's—farm, and Robin remembered it from her years visiting them.

> It was built under the house with an entrance outside on the side of the house. It was dark, with dirt walls and a dirt floor, and had shelves to hold the stored food. It was frightening to me with the idea in my head of bugs and animals, but fortunately I never had to go inside; I just

looked in from the doorway.

Lula's son Dean had memories of tornadoes when Denny was very young:

> Denny was real small and they were all at the farm outside Howard, Kansas. Em came to me and said he had an important job for me to do and wanted me to pay particular attention to what he was saying. Well, I was all ears and wanted to do anything he asked. The farm sat perhaps a hundred feet up the lane from the road, which ran north and south. It was on the east side of the road. The house faced west, and we always entered the house from the rear as you came up the lane from the road to the rear of the house. Immediately to the rear of the house was a cellar that was built half below ground and was entered down the stairs about fifteen feet from the door at the back of the house. At the end of the cellar at the foot of the door was a large bell—the dinner bell, as it was used to call whoever was out in the fields to the house.

> Em pointed out the dark, funny cloud in the west shaped as a funnel and explained that I was to keep one eye on that cloud because it was appearing to be the start of a tornado. Iva Mae was cooking dinner, and he was milking cows in the barn, which was about fifty yards northeast of the house. Iva Mae brought bedding and blankets down, and we put them in the cellar, and she said she would grab Denny and come running the minute I rang the bell. Well, I was geared up and ready, and I thought I understood everything I could possibly need to do my job.

> Perhaps not! Em went to milk the cows. Iva Mae was

cooking the dinner. I was on guard. I would bang that bell as soon as the tornado came close. But when would it be close? Perhaps as soon as it came this way or maybe when it starts up the road? But I decided that as soon as it left the road and started up the lane to the house that it was close enough.

Well, the clouds were perhaps two or three minutes away when Em and Iva Mae went to work. It didn't seem to move real fast at first, but then the dust started to kick up strong and a few trees and shrubs could be seen and were starting to approach the road, and abruptly the tornado veered to the north.

Fantastic, I thought: my job was over and there was nothing to worry about. Just that terrible noise and all that lumber floating around. Then all of a sudden two trucks roared into the lane honking the horn and raising all kinds of hell, yelling for Em. So Em comes from the barn, and Iva Mae comes a-running out of the house, and everybody looks at me still setting on the cellar, hand still on the bell ready to ring it if it just gets close enough.

Maybe not close enough to ring the bell, but close enough to demolish a barn and a couple outbuildings from the ranch that was about a quarter of a mile to the north.

Neither Iva Mae nor Em were happy with me that night, and I don't think either of them cared to hear that I was waiting for it to come closer.

Iva Mae Wyant wedding photo

Chapter 17

R anching was a hard business back in the 1940s and must not have been that profitable. Em and Iva Mae as well as their neighbor, Harry Shepler, sold their ranches. The Sheplers decided to start a retail business buying out a harness shop in Wichita. Known today as Sheplers, the company is well known for country-and-western clothing and accessories. Em and Iva Mae bought a farm near Oak Valley, Kansas. Oak Valley is a township and at the time had a population of twenty-seven. The nearest big city was Longton. The farm was a half mile off the main road. A small, five-room rectangular house, it had a screen door at the kitchen with an old wooden icebox right outside and then a smokehouse and cellar not forty feet away. An outhouse was downhill about a hundred feet from the house. The house itself had a kitchen, dining room, living room, and two bedrooms. It had a front porch, but Denny doesn't recall anyone ever using it other than he and his dad going out and peeing off the porch every night before going to bed.

This working farm did not have electricity. Kerosene and white gas were used for lighting the house, and an old battery-powered radio was used to listen to farm reports and shows like *The Lone Ranger*. The outbuildings included a smokehouse where Iva Mae did the washing out by the fire with a large, old, black cast-iron kettle and a washing machine that was arm operated with squeezers for wringing out the clothes. Up the hill was a chicken house and a barn for their milk cows. This working farm was different from ranching. Dairy cows had to be attended to every day for milking at five in the morning and five in the evening. The cows were milked by hand mainly by Em, with Iva Mae helping. Later they were able to get a gas-powered machine to milk the cows and Em was able to do it all himself.

Attending to the dairy cows and chickens were not the only responsibilities that Em and Iva Mae had to shoulder. This was also a grain farm, with all the work of planting and harvesting. Given that they had more than a hundred acres for seasonal crops such as wheat, corn, alfalfa, and soybeans, the days were full all year long.

During harvest season Em drove the combine while Iva Mae drove the truck. Since they also had hired help to bring in the harvest, Iva Mae would be busy cooking the big noon dinner meals to feed the crew. It's been said that they did not have any trouble finding help to work on the farm because Iva Mae was such a good cook. This was important since many farms needed help at the same time of the year, and the crews picked the places based on the food that would be served.

During this time Iva Mae became pregnant with Sandy. According to her recollections in later years, she was much more careful about watching her weight so she wouldn't have such a hard time giving birth. The countryside was changing, and one of those changes was the addition of electricity. The Rural Electrification Administration, a government agency that provided loan programs, brought electrical and telephone lines to rural areas, and for the first time, Em and Iva Mae had a ceiling lightbulb and electrical outlets in every room. This was a big change in lifestyle during years of great joy and hardships. The electricity meant getting a refrigerator and not having to use oil lamps for light. Still, washing was done outside by hand, and the kitchen appliances were not electric.

Denny had memories of this time before his sister was born:

> This is all BS. *BS* means "Before Sandy," when there was no competition for time and attention and [there was] only one king of the house. So this story, BS, took place in the Flint Hills of Kansas in the mid- and late forties. It was after we left Howard and moved to the farm north of Oak Valley. It was here that lessons of life were taught and that the value of education was understood by both former teachers, Mom and Dad.
>
> Life lessons, like you learned not to name young calves since you would be having them for dinner sometime in

the next year. And you could take a vacation as long as it started after you milked the cows in the morning and ended by the time they needed milking that evening.

I can remember seeing the hurt in Mom's face when a spring flood destroyed our crops and potential income for the year ahead, but I can remember the joy on her face when we got electricity in the house. Still had an outhouse and no running water, but we could play the new radio without the worry that the batteries would soon lose power. Yet those nights without electricity are some of my fondest memories. Since we had to save the radio batteries, Mom would read to me using coal oil lamps.

It was Mom and Dad's interest in education that shaped my early childhood and ultimately molded my future. When the old Hickory Creek one-room schoolhouse was to be torn down, Mom and Dad must have brought at least fifty books from its small library. Mom read every one of those books to me and some of them more than once. The parables from some of these stories became a part of my public speaking career later in life.

Mom and Dad also brought a world globe that day that was hung by a pulley from the ceiling in my room. From it, I studied the world and made promises to explore the lands and travel to the countries I saw. Many years later, Mom traveled with me to some. This is only one of hundreds of stories that was BS, but one with special meaning for me.

Sandra Jean was born on February 24, 1949. Em, Iva Mae, and Denny went twenty-five miles to the closest hospital in Independence, Kansas. It was a Catholic hospital, and according to Denny, it was a dark, dreary, quiet place with the smell of formaldehyde and ether. Hospital stays during that time were longer and much more restrictive. But once Iva Mae and Sandy were released, five-year-old Denny insisted on carrying Sandy out of the hospital and was allowed to do so. Iva Mae in later years said she was praying that Denny would not drop her.

The farm was not doing well during these years. Iva Mae said Em was getting tired and his health was starting to fail. The final blow came when the dairy cattle began to get sick and some died. It started with a cow that would stumble, fall, and get back up to start the same series again. Many of the cows died and had to be carted away. During that time, the blame was put on the new electrical lines that had been installed. In later years when the "mad cow" scare was in the news, Iva Mae believed they had had the same problem on the farm.

Iva Mae would always connect a news story or a place she traveled to with something of her own, whether an experience in her past or a place she had lived. It became a family joke in later years, because no matter where she went, or what she saw or did, she somehow connected it with her hometown.

Unfortunately this was a devastating blow and brought Iva and Em to a crossroads. Up to this point they had been a pretty prosperous middle-class couple. They lost most of their dairy cows, resulting in a turning point in their marriage and a deterioration of Em's health and outlook. He was never the same.

ROBIN ANNE GRIFFITHS

Chapter 18

With Em's health failing, the couple sold the farm and moved to Oak Valley, where they bought a gas station, grocery store, and post office, and moved into a house less than a mile away from the business. The two-story clapboard house had a living room, bedroom, and kitchen downstairs and two bedrooms upstairs. It also had an outhouse, tornado cellar, and some sheds for chickens and sheep.

With a small population of thirty-four, the village of Oak Valley in southeast Kansas on US Route 160 was on the Atchison, Topeka and Santa Fe railway and had a small depot. The Elk River ran through the edge of the town, and before the Depression and the Dust Bowl years, Oak Valley had been fairly prosperous with a string of stores, an old post office, and a feed store. When Em and Iva Mae moved there with Denny and Sandy, the stores had long been gone and the abandoned buildings had only broken windows and empty memories. The town center had moved to the edge of the village between the river and the old stores.

That meant that Em and Iva Mae's new home and business was simply a small country store with two gas pumps fairly alone on US 160. The store was the halfway point between Elk City and Longton, which were about twenty miles apart. It was an old store with two outhouses behind it with "Ma" and "Pa" signs, which travelers on US 160 were thankful to find. With no electricity in the old two-story building, the place was either very hot in the summer or extremely cold in the winter with only a potbellied stove for heat. Electricity did come through during these years and was installed through the Rural Electrification Administration program, which gave the opportunity to have refrigerated products in the store.

Iva Mae applied for the appointment of postmaster for the office in Oak Valley and took the oath at the age of twenty-nine in March 1951. The post office was in the small country store, which became the center of the family's life. Sandy was now a toddler, and she and Denny could spend time in the store during the working day.

Iva Mae fondly recalled one of her favorite stories

about Sandy.

Sandy was one of those babies that climbed before she walked. She whistled before she talked, and she was never still. When she was about three years old, we were running a filling station, grocery store, and post office in Oak Valley, Kansas. We had a bunch of loafers in the store, especially around mail time. They sat around the old coal stove and spit tobacco while talking and teasing Sandy. She wasn't fat but short and chunky. They would say, "Sandy, when are you going on a diet?" and Sandy would say "Soon." They would ask, "Sandy, what are you going to take on your diet?" and Sandy would reply, "Fried chicken and chocolate cake."

Em and Iva Mae were busy daily. Because of the location of the store, along with the post office, a steady stream of people were in and out getting fuel, postage, or basic store items from soap to sodas, which the locals referred to as "soda pop." The mail was delivered by train each morning, and Iva Mae was paid a hundred dollars a month for being the postmaster. Em was her assistant and received forty to sixty dollars a month. This was most of their income at the time, and it was a huge blow when a review of federal spending was taken in Washington and the post office was closed. It wasn't long after the closing of the post office that the store was unable to stay in business. The Oak Valley residents would now need to go to Longton six miles away for larger purchases.

It had been about three years since they had sold the farm and moved to Oak Valley. During those years Iva Mae became unhappy. Later in life, her memories concerning Em were always about his drinking too much. She would occasionally say something about her years with him, their parties, and the drinking crowd they were part of at the time. She even admitted drinking and trying cigarettes, but her character always leaned on the conservative side. Her driving force moved her further away from anyone who didn't see life the way she did. It's easy to imagine how difficult it must have been for them to endure so many losses during those years. After they had lost the post office job and the general store went downhill, Em sold the house. Iva Mae and Sandy moved to Kansas City, where Iva Mae found work, and Em and Denny moved to Longton, Kansas.

Chapter 19

I va Mae did not talk much of her years in Kansas City after leaving Em and Denny. There is a little mystery about these years, since Iva Mae would usually tell anything to anyone, especially if she found it funny although it may have been embarrassing to another person. There was a big age difference between Em and Iva Mae. They had both been through years of struggle financially and emotionally. They grew apart and were arguing more often than not. There were rumors of Iva Mae being with other men in the couple's life. But this will always be a mystery. Finally the end came, and Iva Mae and Em went to the courthouse after filing for divorce and having it granted. Denny saw them both come out with tears in their eyes.

Iva Mae was a survivor. She always looked at what she was doing as the best she could at the time. She would comment many times in her life that she had made her decisions based on what she thought were the right things to do. Many times she would say, "If I had known, I would have done it differently."

In 1953 she left for Kansas City and found a place to live with Em's sister. Sandy was living with Iva Mae's sister Mary and her husband, Homer, on their farm in southern Missouri. In later years, Sandy would comment that she would be very upset when her mom would leave after a visit. The farm in southern Missouri was a long way from Kansas City, and Sandy was just four years old and Denny was ten. Denny was his father's boy and stayed with his dad. He would write to Iva Mae once in a while, and visited her a few times in Kansas City. He often felt it was his fault that his parents had split up, because one of their arguments was over a dog that he wanted, and his dad had gotten it for him. It would be easy to imagine that both Denny and Sandy had feelings of abandonment.

This was a decade of change for America. Transportation by train was fading, and the automobile revolution along with the beginning of the interstate highway system altered the look of cities as well as the countryside. The Cold War between the Soviet Union and the United States had created tension and fear, resulting in suspicion with the anti-communist scare. A sense that everyone had to belong, to conform and fit in, was common. Wives were expected to be home with their children, with husbands earning a living and providing for their family. Divorce was not common and often carried a stigma.

Iva Mae found a job working as a comptometer operator for an oil company for the next three years. Comptometers were the first commercially successful key-driven mechanical calculators. They were amazing machines for the time, and to be skilled and work as an operator was almost considered glamorous. While she was living and working in Kansas City, Iva Mae was on her own again. She was good at her job and had begun to start a new life when she met William Robert Hodge, whom most people called Bob.

Bob was a railroad worker and could talk to anyone about anything on just about any subject. He was twelve years older than Iva Mae, born in 1910, although many of the facts and dates of Bob's life are fuzzy, since he did not share information readily and in many cases may have lied. Right at six foot, Bob was a rugged, slender man with dark brown hair and closely placed blue eyes that could penetrate a person. He had a limited education but loved the outdoors, especially fishing and hunting. He enjoyed baseball as a sport and listened to his favorite teams play on the radio for most of his life. His father, who passed away at the age of seventy-six, was from Tennessee, and his mother, who outlived her husband by several years, was from Arkansas. The family settled in Arkansas, and Bob grew up there with his three younger sisters. Married young, he divorced after what has been said to be a twenty-five-year marriage, during which he had three children who were grown and lived in Arkansas. Bob had little to do with his birth family or his children from his first marriage.

Iva Mae never talked about how she met Bob, about their dating, or anything else related to him. Like her divorce from Em, it was a mystery. Iva Mae was always looking for security and protection, so it's easy to speculate that she was looking to get married again so she would feel secure.

Bob and Iva Mae were married in 1956. She did not keep a copy of the marriage certificate or a written record of the marriage date in her papers. Once married, they moved to the southern part of Missouri to be close to her sister Mary. Sandy was back with her mom, but Denny was still with his dad, whose health continued to fail. Iva Mae started working as a cook and waitress, work she did in many areas over the years, serving her meals to countless folks in southern Missouri.

Bob and Iva Mae's marriage seemed to be set up for failure from the beginning. Bob was going from job to job, and they argued often. They also moved often because of Bob's continual search for a job. Iva Mae became pregnant, and in May 1957, Robin Anne was born. Iva Mae recalled Robin's first years:

> Robin was one of those babies that you had to hold all the time. She wanted attention and she got attention. She had beautiful eyes and was a delight. She sat alone at four months, walked at seven months, and potty trained before she was a year old. I can't remember exactly what she talked about, but she was talking on the telephone by six months. We had one trouble and that was getting her to give up her bottle. I was working, so Mary kept her, and I wouldn't take her bottle as she was two years old and I didn't think she needed it. Homer would get in the car

and go get the bottle. I finally got rid of the bottles, and Homer and Mary told her that Bush, a neighbor, threw them in the river. She never did like Bush.

In November 1957, Denny found his father lying on the sofa one morning. When he spoke, his speech was slurred, but he could be understood. Em told his son to fix his breakfast and go on to school. Being a young boy, Denny did as he was told, thinking nothing of it, but about midmorning, he was taken out of class and told that his father had been taken to the VA hospital in Wichita, Kansas. Not knowing who had helped his father since they had no phone, he wondered how his dad had gotten help, plus he felt guilty that he hadn't alerted someone.

The next morning, at fourteen years old, Denny drove himself the hundred miles to Wichita, to the VA hospital. He asked to visit his father and was told that children under sixteen had to be accompanied by an adult. Denny was not going to let that stop him. He managed to see his father one last time while he was alive. He could not understand what he was saying, but Em was trying very hard to communicate something to Denny. Denny was frustrated, because he couldn't make out the words or meaning. Em died within a couple of days and was buried on a Sunday afternoon. Denny was presented with one of his proudest possessions, the military flag from his father's casket, which has forty-eight stars. Denny then left Longton and moved to the Ozarks in southern Missouri to live with his mom, sisters, and stepfather.

Iva Mae never talked about love, but when she talked about Em, she said he had taken care of her and taught her how to do many things that helped her in life. She focused more on the good from that time in her life than the bad, and from all indications, she loved him. But Iva Mae still was the youngest child and very much wanted her way. When she got a belief in her head, she was very stubborn and not easily changed. Later in life her only negative comment about Em was that he drank too much.

Chapter 20

L ife in the Ozarks in southern Missouri was volatile at best. The family moved there to be close to Iva Mae's sister Mary. Bob was frequently looking for a job, so they moved often. Iva Mae worked all the while in a variety of jobs. She was always a worker. Perhaps it was her farming upbringing or perhaps it was out of fear, but she worked many jobs to make sure she took care of her family. She worked in a shoe factory and in an egg plant. She also had many cooking and waitressing jobs, a few of them on Route 66. Many times she would be working a three-to-eleven or an eleven-to-seven shift. She was juggling a busy schedule, all for the going rate of a dollar an hour. Iva loved recognition and was always proud if she got a tip while waitressing, especially one that was a buck and a half.

All the while she kept her home, fed her family, and did her best as a working woman in the late fifties before the women's movement had begun. Iva Mae counted on her family to help. Sandy was still young but was given the responsibility of taking care of Robin much of the time.

When Denny moved in with them after his father died, they all lived in a small, old, gutted downtown store shaped like a shoe box on Main Street in Hartville, Missouri. The front of the building was the town telephone switchboard, and Iva Mae was the telephone operator. The rest of the building was divided by cardboard boxes for the bedrooms and living area. At the back of the building was a small kitchen with running water. None of the stores in downtown Hartville had indoor plumbing. All had outhouses that were lined up in the back of the buildings.

Telephone operators in the 1950s ran switchboards by connecting calls with phone plugs into the appropriate jack. Each plug was part of a cord circuit with a switch associated that let the operator participate in the call. An operator's assistance was required to connect the calls, and because they were in control of the connection, they were also in a position to listen to private conversations.

We were living in a small trailer at Mary and Homer's. It was too small for all of us, and Bob was out of work as usual. He had got fired from his railroad job. I began searching the paper for a job. I had been working at Republic at a restaurant on the midnight shift, but I couldn't sleep in the daytime. Robin was about five months old, and she didn't sleep in the daytime unless you held her.

They wanted a telephone operator at Hartville, and you could live in the building. So I wrote to them and talked to them on the phone and got the job. I didn't know one thing about being an operator, but I thought I could go down to Hurley a few times and learn. Well, I went once and I took the flu that was so popular in 1957. I was really sick and never did get back to Hurley before we had to move.

We moved in just before I had to take over the night shift. You can guess it: the first call I had was a long-distance one. Fortunately there was a person there to help that night who told me how to ring Lebanon, another town in Missouri. I got through, thanks to that person.

Being a telephone operator was different at that time of life. Everyone would ring Central and then you rang the person they wanted. The telephone office we lived in was something else. It had a utility room, kitchen, and you had to be careful when you walked or you went through the floor. Then there was a bedroom where the telephone office was, and we put our bed in there. Robin wouldn't sleep by herself, so she slept with us by the office.

The local judge had a girlfriend in California, so he would call her about one o'clock in the morning, I guess so his wife wouldn't know. I would just get to sleep and have to get up, and then while they talked, I had to keep awake with nothing to do, so why not listen.

The banker was an alcoholic. He would call and say "Six one," which he didn't say very plain. I finally understood that it was his home. And there was an attorney who got so many calls, especially on Monday mornings. I would've never made it if not for Denny and Sandy. Sandy was in the third grade, but she cooked and helped with Robin. She was so dependable. Denny also was good to help with Robin. One time she had dirty pants, but between Denny and Sandy, they got her changed. We didn't have much money, so we had lots of bologna sandwiches, rabbit, and squirrel, which Bob hunted. Then I made a lot of sorghum cookies.

We used the outside bathroom with the hardware store. It was quite an experience. The morning Sandy started to school, Bob took her, but she came home by herself and got lost. A woman brought her to the door, and she was crying, and I felt so bad. Why didn't I make Bob go get her? He was just loafing.

One Sunday afternoon while living in Hartville, we smelled smoke, and it was the hardware store next door that was on fire. There was just a wall between our place and the hardware store. My mind began to race, because I had to call all the firemen plus other places to come and fight the fire. I was thinking of all the explosives next door—paint, cleaning fluid, etc. I called the Sponslers first, as he was the owner. I told Sandy to get some diapers and bottles and take Robin to the car. Bob and Denny went to fight the fire. I was worried sick about

Denny. He was just fourteen and would get in the middle of the fire. After I called all of Hartville's firemen, they told me they needed more help. So I called the firemen in the neighboring towns of Lebanon, Mountain Grove, and Mansfield.

All the time I was worrying about Denny, Sandy, and Robin. I was also worrying about me. What if something blew up and I couldn't get out? Smoke was getting pretty thick. These were old buildings. Hartville was an old town. Up on the hill they had a big house. They used to hide slaves up there during the Civil War. On the top floor they even had a lookout.

For a while, they didn't think they could stop the fire. But at last they got it calmed down. Finally I got to go outside and clear my lungs. Everything got calmed down with someone to watch for more fire. The hardware store was a mess, and it took quite some time before they could open again. We had to air out our apartment so we could sleep in it. But all ended good, because we were all okay and no one else was hurt. We stayed here till almost spring. The managers kept yelling that we were using too much gas to keep warm. Robin was just a baby, so I told them to get someone else and walked off. We moved to a place at the edge of town till school was out, then moved back to Hurley. We sold the trailer and leased a filling station at Hurley, but that is another story.

ROBIN ANNE GRIFFITHS

Chapter 21

From Hartville the family moved to Hurley. The family lived in several houses that could more accurately be referred to as shelters rather than homes. One did not have electricity, and water was piped from a nearby spring. It did not have indoor plumbing or an outhouse, so each family member picked a part of the woods as their private bathroom space.

Hurley was formerly known as Spring Creek Mill, and a mill of the same name was built on the banks of the creek that ran through the town in the late 1800s. In Hurley Bob leased a local service station. Here they lived in an old house where a son had murdered his father. Because of that tragedy, the place was believed to be haunted, and its reputation made it available to Iva Mae and Bob for only twenty-five dollars a month.

At one point years later, Iva and Denny counted and realized the family had had seventeen different addresses by the time Denny graduated high school.

The family moved to Crane, Missouri, at one point, and Bob leased another gas station in Aurora, Missouri. Denny transferred from the Crane High School to the school in Aurora, where he lived and worked out of the station. The rest of the family remained in Crane until they could find a place to live in Aurora.

Iva Mae became pregnant at age thirty-eight, and Bob was not too happy about it, as she was sick a lot. The relationship between Iva Mae and Bob continued to deteriorate. The stories about Iva Mae's pregnancy are another vague area, and the facts aren't clear. But later in life Iva Mae said that Bob brought her some medicine that she thought was from her doctor. Only after she had taken the dosage did she find out it was from a veterinarian. Bob's version was that she came up with the idea to abort the baby by taking pills that abort puppies, but her family doesn't believe she was ever quite that calculating or cold. The medication she took did make her very ill, and Bob refused to take her to the hospital. Denny ended up taking her, and in October 1960, the day before Denny's seventeenth birthday, Tammy Sue was born but with a birth defect. She didn't have a rectum and had corrective surgery just days after her birth. The medication that Iva Mae took has not been proved to be the cause of the defect, which appears to be a common occurrence in many children. But the damage in Iva Mae and Bob's relationship had deepened, and their relationship took a tragic and downward spiral.

Tammy was born on October 26. The doctor walked into Iva Mae's room and said, "You have a red-headed baby girl, and that is the good news. The bad news is she doesn't have an anal opening." Tammy was taken to St. John's Hospital in Springfield, Missouri, for treatment. She was there for more than six weeks, her life hanging in the balance because of the surgeries. Later in life, Iva Mae told Tammy how hard it was for her, staying in the hospital and having to entertain Tammy to keep her still. The hospital was run by nuns. Iva Mae had to wear a dress every day and take showers in the basement with the nuns. She didn't have a place to sleep other than a little sofa. For some unknown reason, later in Tammy's life Iva Mae thought she needed to know that she had almost been aborted because of her father. It's not known if Iva Mae was trying to deal with her own guilt or lay the blame elsewhere, but the result was a poor lifelong relationship between mother and daughter.

ROBIN ANNE GRIFFITHS

Chapter 22

B ob and Iva Mae moved back to Hurley when Denny
was in his senior year of high school. He had earned a
college scholarship to play basketball and joined the
navy, and would be active after graduation. Once Denny was in
college in Parsons, Kansas, he found work at a turkey factory.
Over the years Denny had worked on turkey ranches, catching
birds for shipment to the processing plant. In Parsons he
secured a job at the local processing plant that paid a dollar and

forty cents an hour. This was good money at the time, and Denny thought he could get Bob and Iva Mae work there as well.

By this time Bob and Iva Mae had worked many odd jobs at different places, including egg plants, gas stations, shoe factories, feed stores, and twenty-four-hour truck stops on the interstate, but they had never earned this high of a wage. The plant hired them without an interview, and Bob and Iva Mae with twelve-year-old Sandy, four-year-old Robin, and one-year-old Tammy moved overnight to Parsons. They settled into a small, furnished apartment over a little diner that cost ten dollars a week. Bob and Iva Mae worked separate shifts. They were able to manage more with the help of Iva Mae's sister and her husband, Lula and Roy, who lived in Parsons. Iva Mae would go to Lula's to do their laundry in an old washtub with a hand wringer and then hang the clothes on the line in their backyard. It was a constant juggling of time, and although the factory provided good-paying jobs, the work was not pleasant, and each day they would leave with the stench of the place on them.

The move and job lasted only a short while before they all quit. Bob and Iva Mae then moved back to the Ozark Mountains and into the extra house that Mary and Homer, Iva Mae's other sister and brother-in-law, owned on their eighty acres. Iva Mae began working in a diner, which gave her the dream of someday having her own restaurant.

Iva Mae and Bob were always on the go for one reason or another. Living in the country meant a trip to do anything. Once on their way home, Iva Mae was driving, which she always did. Bob didn't like to drive with her, and she didn't like his driving. Sandy and Robin were sitting in the backseat with Tammy standing in the middle between them. Sandy was sitting behind her mother, and no one was wearing seat belts because the car did not have any. The countryside was rolling hills, and Iva Mae was traveling around seventy miles per hour. The car almost seemed airborne at times, and Robin would feel herself rising as they dipped in and out of the hills. As they came over one hill, they saw a car with a trunk full of bricks stopped in the road at the bottom of the hill. Iva Mae hit the brakes, but the car was going too fast, and they hit the back of the stopped car. The impact was so hard that it threw Bob and Iva Mae's car back up the side of the hill and everyone forward.

Everyone was quite shaken. Bob's head had hit the windshield and was bleeding. Sandy had thrown out her arms to keep Tammy and Robin in the seats. Robin had fallen to the floor and was going to have a black eye from hitting the door handle. Tammy was shaken and crying but unhurt. Sandy was thrown into the seat back in front of her. Between Sandy hitting the seat and the impact of hitting the car in front of them, Iva Mae was hurt pretty badly. Another vehicle came upon the scene and rushed over to a nearby farm to call for an ambulance. Iva Mae was rushed to the hospital with several broken ribs and other minor injuries. Although she stayed in the hospital for a couple of days, it was not long before she was back on her feet and going to work. They needed the money, and she knew that it was up to her to provide.

At forty-nine, Bob began to exhibit problems. He became suspicious and increasingly agitated, and had spells of anger. As he grew more nervous, Iva Mae became more impatient, and the mix became volatile. Bob suffered more and more from insomnia, tantrums, and paranoia. He was losing weight and becoming unreasonable. Finally he was convinced that he needed help and was admitted to St. John's Hospital in Springfield for about a month with the belief that he was suffering from a nervous breakdown. Once he was released from the hospital, his symptoms worsened.

Bob and Iva Mae had many arguments that would turn violent, with items in the house being thrown. Bob began to have unexplained spells of anger that grew longer until one episode fused with the next. He slept with a knife and pistol and would threaten to use them on Iva Mae and the family. He became cruel in punishing the children and had ideas of being persecuted. He would spend long spans of time just sitting and staring at nothing. The episodes continued to escalate over the next two years until he worked only part of the time. The sickness was consuming him, and Iva Mae was afraid for herself and the children.

One morning arguing erupted between them, and Bob was holding Tammy in a way that was frightening. Iva Mae grabbed Tammy out of his arms, and as she sat her down, Bob grabbed Iva Mae and put a knife to her throat, telling her he was going to kill her. He even threatened to rape his stepdaughter, Sandy. Five-year-old Robin, who witnessed the whole thing, ran out of the house and continued the quarter mile down the rocky dirt road to Mary's to get help. As she ran up the driveway to the house, she found Mary and while catching her breath told her that her daddy was hurting her mommy. Mary grabbed her hand and they started the walk back, not knowing what had happened or what they would find.

As they came up the hill to the driveway, they saw Bob's car heading down the road. Mary and Robin ran into the house to find Iva Mae and Tammy shaken but all right. Iva Mae knew that Bob needed help and that she could not trust that everything would be okay if something didn't change.

Iva Mae Hodge

Chapter 23

B
ob knew that something was wrong. Once he returned
to the house, Iva Mae told him that she and the
children could not have him around because he was
acting crazy and they were afraid of him. She had called and
talked to the doctors who had treated him in the hospital
earlier that year, and they recommended that he voluntarily
admit himself into the Nevada State Hospital in Nevada,
Missouri. He agreed to go, and at fifty-one, nervous, having

tantrums, and suffering from insomnia, he made the trip with
Iva Mae to check himself into the facility.

The Nevada State Hospital was established in 1885 and was
the third asylum in Missouri. It was known by several names,
including Insane Asylum Number 3, Lunatic Asylum Number
3, and later, State Hospital Number 3. It was a massive
building, and when completed in 1887 it was the largest single
building in the state. It was built in the distinctive Second
Empire style and had an ornate facade. The large structure
spread over a mile in circumference on a large parcel of land.
The building had several towers and included its own
dormitories, a dairy, a hennery, massive storage areas, and
a cemetery.

Bob checked into the hospital in July 1962. He was interviewed
and examined by hospital staff for mental instabilities, resulting
in this report:

> This fifty one year old white married male had a high
> school education, worked at plumbing and painting, and
> was the father of five children. Patient reported as
> suspicious, threatened suicide and had spells of anger.
> Patient alleged to have threatened the life of his relatives
> and threatened to rape his stepdaughter. He also was
> reported to have suffered from insomnia, slept with a
> knife and pistol under pillow, etc. Patient is a voluntary
> admission. He is related to several prominent men in our
> territory—sheriff, deputy sheriffs, etc. He says he was
> born in Mt. Pleasant, Tennessee, attending the local
> schools through the eleventh grade. He also states he had
> the usual childhood diseases. He had no serious illness
> any time, neither a serious injury, until he was wounded in

the left knee while in the military service. A bullet went through the knee. It has left no crippling defects.

The patient states that he belongs to the American Legion, Veterans of Foreign Wars and the Independent Order of Odd Fellows. He has been active in local politics. He also states that he is a plumber and painter; he is married with four children. He does not drink but smokes about one pack of cigarettes daily. The examiner believes his psychomotor activity is normal. He is friendly, talks freely and does not appear to cover up or withhold information. Affect is one of frankness. Ward notes described patient as quiet, cooperative, and somewhat nervous but got along well on the ward.

Diagnostic Summation: We have a fifty one year old man, apparently in good physical condition. He comes to us because of insomnia, nervousness, and temper tantrums, voluntarily—knowing that he needs help. He is of an age that you might wonder if he is an involutional psychotic. His trouble is of such short duration. Again you might wonder if he was toxic—acute brain syndrome. The examiner is more of the opinion that he comes nearer being a Psychoneurotic Disorder, Depressive Reaction. Diagnosis: Psychoneurotic Disorder, Depressive Reaction.

During the six months Bob was in the hospital, Iva Mae continued to work and live in Crane. She visited Bob occasionally with Robin and Tammy. During his treatment, Bob was given opportunities to do woodworking and other crafts to occupy his time and help with treatments. In the hospital he was agreeable and pleasant to the staff and did not seem to exhibit the same signs that had brought him there. During a visit, Iva Mae agreed to Bob spending weeks at home if the doctor authorized that he was ready. Bob was transferred to an open ward and then eventually discharged.

Once Bob returned home, things had changed and he decided to take action. The results were front-page news in the *Stone County Republican* paper in May 1963. Iva Mae was photographed pointing to an order prohibiting her from removing anything from her home in Crane. The order was signed by the Stone County sheriff.

> Stone County Sheriff T. J. Walker took the administration of justice in his own hands again last week when he signed an order prohibiting a Crane woman from removing anything from her own home.

> Mrs. W. R. Hodge found the notice on her front door when she returned from a trip early last week. She is the mother of three children ages two, five and fourteen. The notice, typed on the Sheriff's official stationery, informed her that she was to remove nothing from her home.

> Mrs. Hodge was intending to move but was afraid to touch anything because of the notice. She said she consulted a prominent Springfield attorney and was told that the Sheriff had absolutely no legal right to issue such a notice and that he could help her if she lived anywhere but Stone County. He informed her that justice was impossible with the present law enforcement in the county and that the only thing he could do was advise her to move to another county.

> With the help of Crane officials and friends Mrs. Hodge

defied the order and moved her belongings out of the house. The notice stated that the order was taken by order of the Prosecuting Attorney. Stone County Prosecutor said he did not even discuss the matter with the Sheriff before the notice was posted. He said that the Prosecutor had no right to issue such an order any more than the Sheriff had. The only person with authority for such an order would be a judge. The judge would have to issue and sign such an order and then the only part the Sheriff would play in the matter would be to serve the papers. No papers were served at all in this instance, however. The notice was posted on the door of the house. It is not known as yet whether any action will be taken against the Sheriff for signing the order.

Iva Mae moved the house belongings like a thief in the night with the help of Denny and some friends. In later years she would say that they had hurried so much that many of her family memories and special sentimental items were left in the house and lost forever. The story escalated, and after the article was printed, the sheriff denied signing the order and was quoted by at least one area daily newspaper and one metro television station as saying he did not sign the paper. A week later another notice was put into the local paper written by Bob.

To Whom It May Concern: I, W. R. Hodge, want to clarify the statement which in last week's Stone Co. Republican regarding to a notice put on my house in Crane, regarding my personal property which was being sold by my wife while I was in the hospital, when I got home she was gone and not living there. All property was boxed up that I had left. I went to Galena after I found out she wouldn't live with me, to talk to the County Attorney, who told me to put the Notice on the door and have the Sheriff write it out for me and told me what to say on it. One of the Sheriff's Deputies typed it out and I took it to my home and put it on my door. It was for the purpose of each one getting our personal property, the Deputy Sheriff sent by the Sheriff's department and the Mayor of Crane was present when we divided up. Sheriff T. J. Walker had nothing to do with this nor did he or his deputies post it. Sheriff Walkers name was typed on the letterhead. W. R. Hodge, Crane, Missouri.

During this time Iva Mae with the three girls began moving around, living in motels to hide from Bob. She asked an attorney about a divorce and was told she could not get one because Bob was not mentally fit. By March 1963, Bob was back at Nevada State Hospital, but this time he had no choice. Once he was in the hospital, the staff began to evaluate him.

> Mr. Hodge was returned today by the Sheriff and a deputy for whom an order to return the patient was set by the Judge requiring a signature of the return of the patient. The Sheriff said he did not feel that Mr. Hodge was mentally sick, that he had been working since he left here and that the return was instigated by Mrs. Hodge through the Judge.

> The patient tells [us] he has been working every day since he left here. He was surprised when he was served the notice of his being returned by the sheriff. He points out that there was some difficulty in getting Mrs. Hodge to come for him when he was here before. Mrs. Hodge had collected Social Security since he was committed and got

about four hundred dollars back pay besides her monthly amount which she has been receiving up to now but may be in danger of having cut off since he is not any longer employed. Mr. Hodge does not want his wife to be the one to whom we are responsible for his release and has asked that his sister Annie to be the one to whom we should correspond. He says he has been in contact with an attorney about his wife's attitude toward him. I pointed out that he had the right to apply for court review of his case through petition to the Judge of his county. We will observe the man and determine the need for his detention here. I did not see anything unusual about the man, he was very well composed in spite of the plight he tells he is in.

It was not long before Bob was released with the help of his sister Annie. Iva Mae was working as much as she could while Sandy watched Robin and Tammy. They were living in motels and moving often so Bob would not find them. During this time Iva Mae was worried about her children, having enough money to live on, and her marriage. She started praying for an answer. She asked God for help finding a good place to live that would be close to schools, finding a good job to support herself and the kids, and staying safe. If God provided all these things, she said, she would change her life and go to church. While looking for a place to move and a job, she saw an ad for a house in Springfield with a school just down the block.

Iva Mae tried to get a divorce but couldn't because Bob was considered unstable at the time. She made up her mind that if she had to live with him, it was going to be on her terms. The first house she looked at was exactly what she wanted: a small home with a fenced backyard. It was a block from the grade school, and a church was just down the street. The Sunday school teacher lived next door, and he and his wife had two grandchildren who were Robin and Tammy's age. Iva Mae believed that this was God literally answering her prayers. Denny was going into college, Sandy high school, and Robin grade school, and Tammy was almost ready for kindergarten. It was a new beginning.

Chapter 24

In Springfield, the Grant Street rental house was a four-room old wood-framed house with a small, detached one-car garage that was used for storage. The fenced backyard was fairly large, and there was a dead-end street behind it. The front entrance had a small porch with a doorway that led into the living room. The old house had high ceilings and a large old gas heater in the living room. There were two large bedrooms and one bathroom with a tub, toilet, and sink. The kitchen was large enough for a table and chairs, and had old white cabinets and a sink. The gas stove was on the wall next to the cabinets, and a refrigerator stood against the opposite wall. The house had a back porch, which Bob converted into another bedroom. The home was small, clean, and workable.

Denny moved back in and had started college at Southwest Missouri State after graduating junior college in Kansas. He had a job working nights and had the back-porch bedroom. Sandy had started high school at Parkview High and had the front bedroom to the house. Bob and Iva Mae had the bedroom that was off the kitchen with the bathroom. Robin and Tammy slept in that room as well, in a cot and a crib. It was tight, but no one seemed to notice, and for all purposes, it worked.

Springfield, the third-largest city in the state, is known as the birthplace of Route 66. Home to several universities, it is part of the Bible Belt and the gateway to the Ozarks. The rental house that Iva Mae and Bob moved into was in an older neighborhood not far from the downtown area. The homes in the area were built in the early 1920s, and many of the larger houses had been converted to apartments.

Grant Street was a main thoroughfare in Springfield that ran through the downtown and residential areas. The street was busy with traffic, so the neighbors did not mingle with each other on the street side. The side streets were more of a quiet open neighborhood where children played and people gathered. Grant Street did offer entertainment, and a porch swing on the front of the house gave a front row seat to the variety of traffic that moved past on a daily basis. A tamale vendor with a pushcart strolled by once a week. An elderly gentleman who walked very slowly and always dressed in a large overcoat and hat could be seen daily throughout the year in any weather, hot or cold. During the school year children would make the trip to and from the grade school just a block away. Across from the school was a small store that many children would stop in on their way home to buy candy or the latest comic book.

The neighbors living to the north side of the house were Ivan and Mae. Ivan was a deacon and Sunday school teacher for adults at the fundamentalist Baptist church just down the street. He was a gentle soul who in his middle age did not drive or have a driver's license. Children sought him out at the church because he always had small sticks of gum to give each of them on Sundays. Mae was the matriarch of the church who knew everyone and everything. She was always groomed perfectly. Ivan and Mae lived alone, with visits from their only daughter and grandchildren.

As soon as Iva Mae met her neighbors, she decided that she was right and God had led her to move next to them, and she was in church that very next Sunday. Bob was not working, so Iva Mae picked up jobs to keep the household going. She went to the local vocational technical school and received her cook, hotel, and restaurant training and certification. She found families that had children who needed a babysitter, picked up ironing at a dime a shirt, and worked at a school cafeteria. She was determined that life was going to change.

> The first Sunday morning we went to church, we came home to Bob and three other men sitting drinking in the kitchen, and I went to the table and threw away all the beer.

Iva Mae and Bob got into an argument, and she threw a cast-iron skillet at him. It hit the wall, but the result was the end of Bob having anyone at the house to drink or do anything. Bob was defeated at this point and did not want to go back to the hospital. He was becoming quiet and withdrawn, and started to spend more time away and outside. This was the last violent episode between them. They still had arguments, but usually it was Iva Mae upset with Bob and Bob withdrawing after a few words.

> The second Sunday at church I went up and was saved. It was the sixth of October in 1963. I had stopped drinking. I had really stopped. I didn't want anything but God. I stopped cussing immediately. I didn't even want to tell dirty jokes or have anything to do with the life that I had before. But I had wondered if I did it right. I prayed and prayed if I did it right. One night I prayed if I did it right. I was dreaming I was in bed and I thought Jesus was over me in the bed and was beckoning me to come up. I was yelling, "I am coming, I am coming." I woke everyone up in the house. After that I never worried again. I have had Jesus with me all the time.

Iva Mae made friends at the church. She also found a friend in the alley behind her home. June and Bob lived on the street behind them with their three children, a girl who was the same age as Robin and two boys Tammy's age and younger. June and Iva Mae became best friends and did everything together. They talked about everything and supported each other as best friends do with whatever was going on in each other's life. June's husband, Bob, became friends with Iva's Bob. Because of this friendship, Bob joined the local painter's union and started working more often. He even traveled out of town to jobs, which seemed to make Iva Mae happy: she liked having him gone and having an income coming into the household.

The move to Springfield happened just before school started. A few weeks before the first day of school, the neighborhood children were playing in the backyard. They had tied a rope a few inches off the ground from a tree to the fence and were trying to walk across the rope. Robin fell during her turn and twisted her ankle. She was crying and taken into the house and told to rest. Iva Mae thought she had just sprained it and let it go. The next day it was turning colors and had become very swollen. Still, Iva did not believe it was serious. The third day Robin could not put weight on it, so Iva Mae drove to a doctor in Aurora who had helped her before. The doctor told her it was broken and needed to be cast. Iva Mae did not have any money for the medical attention, and the doctor told her to pay what she could when she could and to take care of Robin.

The world was once again changing. The Beatles, the sensational band from England, released "I Want to Hold Your Hand," the civil rights movement was gaining momentum with the leadership from Martin Luther King Jr., Vietnam was becoming troublesome, and in November, President Kennedy was assassinated in Dallas. Iva Mae was attached to the small black-and-white television in their living room as the events unfolded. She had always been interested in the news and kept up with local and national events. The schoolteacher in her was always alert for information. The following spring after the Kennedy assassination, General Douglas MacArthur died. The news carried the funeral on television then as well.

Tammy was barely three when John Kennedy was killed.

There wasn't anything on television except about the Kennedys. I stayed glued to the TV, afraid I would miss something. Saturday morning cartoons were not on because of the news coverage. About three months later on a Saturday morning Tammy ran into the kitchen yelling, "Kennedy done died again." They were having another funeral on television for MacArthur.

The friendship between June and Iva Mae grew. Iva Mae was now forty-one and June was about ten years younger. June was an attractive woman. She was tall and thin with a style of her own. She had dark black hair, which was always in place, as was her clothing and jewelry. June was always babysitting children, as was Iva Mae. They both loved to be on the go and found things to do often where they would load up the car and take off to the Grant Street swimming pool or to all the garage sales they could find. Both would pack lunches and stop at the local park to feed everyone. Neither June nor Iva Mae had much money, but they found a way to entertain themselves and the children for a day. Later in life June's memories of Iva Mae included this one:

> One day she decided she wanted to go see a fortune-teller, just for fun. So we left the kids with Sandy and took off together. The house we went to was awful, with a lot of cats and fleas. The fortune-teller told her that she would move. She also told her that she would never have another man in her life after Bob. Iva Mae was a little disturbed when the fortune-teller told her she saw darkness for her son, Denny. What was so funny is Iva Mae did not want anyone to know that she went, because her Sunday school teacher lived next door to her. We knew the fortune-teller was of the devil.

The other time Iva Mae and I did something together is when she wanted a new dress. We went shopping to a place outside of town called The Dixie. They had dress sizes that were larger and were not easily found at the time. She found the one she wanted and it cost $12.95. She liked it so much, she wore it home. Iva Mae had ironing all week long to pay for the dress. She never had a lot of money and she loved clothes. Iva Mae was an outstanding person and she meant a lot to me.

The family was getting settled and becoming part of the neighborhood. Iva Mae became involved in PTA and was at Robin and Tammy's school events. Sandy had learned to sew and made many of her own clothes, as well as clothes for Robin and Tammy. Sandy's sewing talent meant big savings. Robin and Tammy were dressed alike most Sundays, and Sandy was able to have more clothes for school and church than she would have had otherwise.

Sunday school and church services were a big part of their lives, and even Bob attended occasionally, although not often, because he would be pressured to be saved. The friendships with the neighbors grew, and Iva Mae's house became a central location of all the neighborhood children to play in the backyard or to watch a few of their favorite shows on television on Saturday mornings or early after school. Denny was graduating college on the G.I. Bill and leaving for naval training. Tammy was graduating kindergarten. Sandy had made friends at high school as well as in the young people's group at church. She was also Iva Mae's main help with the children. Bob was gone often but working, so he and Iva Mae didn't have as many conflicts as they had had before.

Iva Mae was feeling a little more comfortable in life and started
to broaden herself by trying new and different things.
Although she worried all her life, she was not as afraid and felt
a little more secure. As a family they were covering their basic
needs and starting to save a little money, but life was still pretty
precarious. Iva Mae had Sandy dye her hair, because she had
been going gray in the front around her forehead from the
time she was nineteen. She had picked a dark solid black for
the color similar to her best friend June's hair, and once it
was done decided it was not for her. She never colored her
hair again.

She never had a flair for or understanding about makeup or
jewelry. She wore just the basics with powder and lipstick and
did not have any interest or confidence in learning more about
technique. Later in life she developed a liking for earrings and
enjoyed matching them to her outfits. Iva Mae had beautiful
skin that was almost porcelain in later years once she was out
of the sun. She had an even tan coloring and big sky blue eyes
that you didn't always notice because of the eyelid folds over
them angled over the sides. Her nose was wide and high, and
she had almost apple cheeks. Her smile was wide and her teeth
were healthy and pretty, and she had a little protruding
rounded chin that ran through her family.

She wanted to lose weight and was always trying a new fad diet.
She went to a "diet doctor" who gave her medication to help
her lose weight. Unfortunately the doctor did not check her
vital signs or anything else. Iva Mae walked out of the house
one morning with a basket full of laundry to hang on the line
in the backyard. As she stepped off the porch, she missed the
step and fell, hitting her arm and breaking it in three places
around the elbow. Rushed to the hospital, she had surgery and

found out that she suffered from hypertension. The medication she had been taking had spiked her blood pressure, and she had been close to having a stroke.

Recovery was difficult but fairly quick with Iva Mae's busy schedule of ironing and taking care of the children she babysat. She relied heavily on Sandy's help. She was unable to use her arm for several weeks, but it only slowed her; she never stopped completely. She and Bob had never had any form of insurance, and many times the doctor bills were forgiven or discounted and paid in little installments over time. With the discovery of hypertension, she began taking medication for her blood pressure, for which she would be treated for the rest of her life.

ROBIN ANNE GRIFFITHS

Chapter 25

As Denny was completing college, he dated many girls and occasionally brought them home. Iva Mae would never have warning of the visits, but it did not seem to bother her other than the one-time visit from a Miss Missouri pageant contestant. Iva Mae began a ritual during these years of changing into her nightgown and robe right after dinner was over and the kitchen was cleaned. It became known as her after-five attire and was an inside joke to her and the family. Many evening visitors met Iva Mae for the first time in her after-five attire. One was Judy, who visited with Denny for the first time after a party where Denny had made a drink called a Purple Cow. The meeting was a little hazy at best. Judy was a smart and beautiful woman and later became Denny's wife. Robin and Tammy both fell in love with her because she was fun and would spend time playing games with them on the floor.

Denny finished college and received his degree. Afterward he was off to start his military career as an officer in naval air. He was in Pensacola, Florida, when Iva Mae received a call that Denny was losing his eyesight because of a training accident. She didn't say much, but hung up the phone and went off to be by herself and cry. Years later she would say that God had taken Denny's eyesight so he would not be killed in the Vietnam War. She also remembered the fortune-teller who had foreseen Denny in darkness. She made the connection but said only that the fortune-teller was a temptation from the devil.

By 1965, Judy and Denny were married and living in Pensacola. The war in Vietnam was continuing to escalate, and the antiwar movement was growing. Civil unrest in areas around the country included rioting, looting, and arson. The miniskirt appeared, and men's hair was getting longer. The space race was in full swing with the start of the Gemini program, and the launch of Gemini 4 was broadcast in color by NBC for the first time. Winston Churchill died, and Malcolm X was assassinated. *The Sound of Music* premiered, and Iva Mae's favorite soap opera, *Days of Our Lives*, began.

Not long after Denny lost most of his sight, with only peripheral vision remaining in both eyes, he medically retired from the navy in 1966 and began a career in the private sector, starting with the National Cash Register Company. Iva Mae decided to visit Denny and Judy in Pensacola. With Robin and Tammy out of school for the summer, she packed for the three of them and took a Greyhound bus from Springfield. It was a long and hard trip with children and included many stops and a few transfers. Iva sat up front near the driver. Tammy sat next to Iva Mae, and Robin was in the seat across the aisle. This worked until a man sat next to Robin and scared her. For the remainder of that trip and the return, Robin sat next to Iva Mae, and Tammy was on her mother's lap.

All went fairly smoothly until they stopped in Mobile, Alabama. Having not slept most of the night on the ride, Iva was tired. Robin and Tammy had slept some but not well. They got off the bus to go into the terminal to have breakfast. Iva was not paying close attention since she was tired and walked into the "colored" section of the bus stop to sit down and order food. Once she realized where she was, she hurried her wide-eyed children out of the room and into the white section of the bus stop to have breakfast.

Once they arrived in Pensacola, the trip became a vacation that no one would forget. Denny and Judy provided visits to the naval air station, which has many interesting and educational areas to do with aviation, training, and the Blue Angels flight squadron. Sightseeing trips included Fort Barrancas and shopping in the tourist district at typical beach-type souvenir stores. The beach of pure white sugar sand was blinding, but the beauty stood out even to Robin and Tammy at their young age.

The trip was completely enjoyable until a full day on the beach and in the water turned Iva Mae's back a bright red. The sunburn was so severe that just having her clothing touch her back was painful. She was miserable and did not have any knowledge of how to treat it, so she suffered. The bus ride back was not pleasant, because Iva Mae was not comfortable, Robin would only sit in the seat next to her, and Tammy rode on her lap. The trip was forever known as the trip that Iva Mae got sunburned. It was a topic of discussion for many years when a beach or Florida came up in conversation.

Chapter 26

School was beginning again, and Sandy had been sewing clothes for herself and the kids during the summer. At age seventeen she had been carrying the responsibilities of an adult for many years. She had several friends through the church group but fewer at school. Her grades were good, she worked part time, and she cared for Tammy and Robin much of the time when Iva was busy with work or other things.

She seldom had a boyfriend, but during this school year she began to date a young man of Mexican descent named Oscar. Oscar was in the army and would soon be leaving for Vietnam. It was a difficult situation, because every time Oscar would come to the house, Bob would stomp out, showing that he did not approve of the young man. He would not speak to the young man, and it made no difference that Oscar was serving his country. As far as Bob was concerned, Oscar was not good for his stepdaughter because of his ethnicity, and that was all there was to it.

Oscar was used to this type of attitude, and although it was uncomfortable, he still came to the house with Sandy when she asked. Iva Mae was polite and tolerant but not happy about the dating. She had grown up with the idea that the races should not mix. When Robin started grade school, she had several classmates who were black. She was making friends and wanted to invite them home. Iva Mae told her, "It's fine to be friends with them, Robin, but you don't want them as your good and close friends." So she thought the same of Oscar.

Sandy was in love with Oscar. She thought he was kind and thoughtful. Sandy had never been the center of attention, and in Oscar's world she was his center. They continued to date even with the strained family feelings until Oscar left for Vietnam. He sent Sandy presents of items he purchased while traveling on the other side of the world. The pressure of him being away and Bob and Iva Mae's disapproval finally won, and they grew apart. Oscar always held a special place in her heart, because he loved her and made her feel special.

The little house on Grant Street was always full. It became the gathering place for all of Robin and Tammy's friends to play in the yard or run in for their favorite television show. Iva Mae was fine with them being there because it kept her children busy and she knew where they were. Sandy had friends from church over occasionally but few friends from school. This was also good with Iva Mae, since she approved of the church friends and did not know the ones from school.

Life had settled down to some extent for the volatile family, and their financial situation was becoming more stable. Iva Mae decided that she wanted her own home and began to look at the possibilities. She and Sandy, with Robin and Tammy in tow, started to search out homes in the area. Bob never was part of the search. Iva Mae and Sandy looked at a wide range of homes, but the goal was to have a big yard and enough bedrooms. It was a big adventure for Robin and Tammy to see the different houses, particularly the thought that they might have a bedroom of their own. One home on the south side of town near the hospital looked to be perfect. In fact it was a dream house for the family: two stories, and much newer and more modern than what they were living in. Iva Mae and Sandy spent one evening going over their meager savings, bonds, coins, and anything else they could use as a down payment. It was not enough, so the search continued.

Finally they found a small home on Main Street near the high school Sandy attended and within walking distance of a beautiful old park named Fassnight. It was a perfect area. It was quiet and an actual neighborhood off the busy streets. The area had a mixture of homes of different values. Most were older ranch-style, one story, with a few two-story homes mixed in. The house was not perfect; it was still small and would need changes made. It had a nice front yard with a one-car driveway leading to an attached garage. The home sat next to an alley that ran down the side of the house, and there was another alley behind the backyard. A walkway led to the front entrance step, which opened to the living room with a large picture window. The living room led into a dining room, which had a hallway to the left leading to a small bathroom and two bedrooms. One bedroom was larger than the other but still small overall. The dining room led to a small kitchen and laundry room and then a garage with a door to the backyard. The backyard was fenced and had a patio area with an old block fireplace grill for cookouts and a small shed to store items such as the lawn mower.

Iva Mae liked the home. It was the right price for their small financial ability and could be made to work. She and Bob signed the deal to buy the place, and Bob began to work on the changes needed to live there. Bob enclosed the garage, turning it into a bedroom for him and Iva Mae; he then painted all the rooms. Sandy was assigned the smaller of the two bedrooms on one end, and Robin and Tammy shared the other. The house was much newer than the rental they had lived in for the past five years. The family ended up living at this home on Main Street longer than they had lived anywhere since Bob and Iva Mae were married.

Everyone felt they were moving into a brand-new home, and there was a sense of excitement about the change. The bathroom was modern, with a shower rather than just an old tub. The kitchen was small and did not have much cabinet space. The laundry room next to the kitchen was a dream come true. Iva Mae would not have to go to the coin-operated laundry again as she had done at least weekly for many years. Bob had been working steadily for the past few years and established a painting and wallpapering business by word of mouth. Iva Mae had continually been taking in ironing and caring for others' children to the point that sometimes she had two or three toddlers and a baby at one time. Life had improved overall, confirming what Iva Mae believed about having God in her life.

It was the end of summer, and Sandy was going into her last year of high school; Robin and Tammy were moving to a new grade school, which was farther away and not within walking distance. Robin was in sixth grade and would soon be moving into junior high. Iva Mae was going to miss living next to her close friend but knew that this was the right thing to do and that her family's life was improving. The neighborhood had a mix of older couples and young families, so she knew they would make new friends and get settled quickly.

The first night after they moved in, the entire family had trouble sleeping because it was too quiet. They had lived so long on a street with a high volume of traffic that not having the sound kept them awake.

ROBIN ANNE GRIFFITHS

Chapter 27

The year was 1968, arguably the most historic year in modern American times. The country was in turmoil with a year that brought a president to not seek reelection, the assassination of Martin Luther King Jr., and the fatal shooting of Robert Kennedy. The peace movement was continuing to grow as more Americans were against the war in Vietnam. Riots occurred in many cities throughout the country as racial tensions continued to mature. The television brought the pictures of the graphic war into the living rooms of America as families were having their evening meals. Pop culture was becoming more daring with music as the Beatles and Rolling Stones led the way, fashion flirted with see-through blouses, and midi- and maxi-skirts were part of the fashion along with the miniskirt. The year saw tremendous change in all aspects of life.

Moving to the little house on Main Street brought many changes for Iva Mae and her family as well. Iva Mae continued to babysit and take in ironing. Bob was busy daily with jobs that he found painting and wallpapering for residential homes and commercial businesses. Robin and Tammy were in a new school, and it was a big change for them both. None of their friends were at this school, so everything was new. It was a big transition and tough for them both. Robin was in her last year of grade school, Tammy was in third grade, and they had to be taken to school and picked up daily.

The neighborhood they lived in was pleasant and they were making new friends, although not the same type of close friends they had had previously. Bob and Iva Mae were on speaking terms with a few of the neighbors but not overly friendly. On one side of their home, a couple had two sons and a daughter. The daughter was Robin's age, and the younger son was Tammy's age. None of the families in this neighborhood had close bonds like the ones in their old neighborhood.

The next door neighbor's house was very close to them, and their garage and the walkway to their backyard was next to Robin, Tammy, and Sandy's bedrooms. Bob and Iva Mae's house did not have air-conditioning, and they used window fans throughout the home to move the summer air. More than once the boys were caught looking in the windows as they passed by. Bob had to have a conversation with their father, but that did not seem to help, so the girls had to be careful when getting dressed.

Iva Mae continued what she had done for many years now on Sundays. She started the day early, getting up to prepare the food for the day. She made breakfast every day for everyone in the family—usually eggs, bacon, and toast for the adults and cereal for the girls, although on Sundays they had a special breakfast of pancakes or French toast. Denny would call most Sunday mornings to talk to his mother and have quick conversations with Robin and Tammy. Every Sunday Iva Mae prepared either a pot roast or fried chicken for Sunday dinner, which was finalized and served right after church services. Then almost every Sunday, she, Robin, and Tammy would take a trip down to the country near Hurley to visit her sister Mary. After the trip and return home, everyone would change back to their Sunday church clothes for evening services. For several years, Sandy came along for the trip to Mary's until she had grown older and was in high school. Bob seldom came along, but occasionally he did when there was a family reunion.

Over the years, family reunions were a big event, with many family members attending. In the early years of Iva Mae's life, the events took place at her sister Lula's home. After Lula passed away, the reunions were mainly at Mary and Homer's farm. Occasionally they would be held at Iva Mae's brother's home. Pete and his wife, Maxine, had two children close to Robin and Tammy's age. The reunions were always fun for the children, because Mary and Homer's farm had many dogs and cats to play with and farm animals to watch. Pete and Maxine's home had many fun things to do such as pony rides and toy train rides. The adults always enjoyed big meals and lots of conversation. Most reunions would include exchanging photos and home movies for all to enjoy.

Mary was a good listener, and Iva Mae would talk about all her problems. Iva Mae always thought Mary was good to her, but she knew, and said, that Mary was wishy-washy and agreed with whomever she was with at the moment.

After one of Iva Mae's visits to see her sister, she returned home to a newly painted dining room. Bob had been busy painting all afternoon. The top half was a cream color, and the bottom half was from the green family, somewhere between lime and sage. Iva Mae took one look and immediately told Bob she didn't like it. Bob, who thought he was doing something special, became angry, and a huge argument began that got completely out of control. There was no violence, but it was loud and hurtful. Robin and Tammy were frightened and disappeared to their bedroom. Sandy was at work and not home. Iva Mae slept in Robin and Tammy's room that night. Bob ended up repainting the room within days, as Iva Mae did not stop berating him about it. The episode showed how thin the relationship between them had become and how much Iva Mae despised Bob.

The incident faded and life continued on, but there was always tension in the house. Bob did not do anything around the house without Iva Mae's expressed wishes and spent most of his time at home in the backyard listening to the radio. He would have conversations with Robin about how much Iva Mae did not like him or how he could not please her. But most of all he told Robin that he did not understand why.

Sandy had been working nights part time at Litton Industries, an advanced circuitry manufacturer company, during her last year of high school. The job helped her pay for her personal expenses and transportation, and contribute to Iva Mae and Bob's household. She continued to make most of her and the children's clothing. Sandy had the opportunity to graduate early, and she took advantage of it so she could work full time. Because of her school grades she was able to enroll in college classes from a scholarship. She, Iva Mae, and the children continued to attend the church on Grant Street. She also was dating occasionally and meeting new friends outside the church's young people's class. For some reason she found she did not want to go to college. She couldn't tell Iva Mae she did not want to continue, so she would leave in the morning and just go to the library to spend the day instead.

Sandy was nineteen years old and floundering. Then one of her dating experiences ended with her becoming pregnant. She had no choice but to tell her mother that she was in trouble. Unwed mothers were presumed to be promiscuous, and a stigma was attached to illegitimate babies. A pregnancy out of wedlock was something to be ashamed of and not to be discussed. Iva Mae took charge and found Sandy a no-frills maternity home in Kansas City where she could wait out the pregnancy and surrender the child for adoption. Sandy had no say in what happened next. Iva Mae was scared someone would find out and people would blame her. Bob looked at his stepdaughter with contempt and called her a whore. He shamed her, and from that moment on, Sandy had only hatred in her heart for him. She was quietly shipped off with few of Iva Mae's friends knowing why, and when anyone inquired, including Robin and Tammy, they were told she was visiting and staying with a cousin.

Sandy had her daughter all alone without any frills. There was no joy in the home, as it was there for one purpose. Once the baby was born, Sandy did not want to give her up but had no choice, and it haunted her. She was brought back to Springfield, and with the help of one of Iva Mae's friends, Sandy found a new job with the railroad. This new job was good because it gave her an opportunity to leave Bob and Iva Mae's home and start her own life with a move to St. Louis. Sandy was finally going to have a life on her own terms without the responsibilities that she had carried for most of her life.

Chapter 28

L ife was once again changing for Iva Mae. It was 1969, and the world was expanding as the first man landed on the moon with the Apollo 11 mission. Richard Nixon became president of the United States, and the world watched as Woodstock attracted hundreds of thousands to an open field to watch some of the most electrifying rock-n-roll musicians of the day.

A new type of store called Kmart was opening in Springfield. The store was completely different at the time, taking the five-and-dime drugstore concept to a large discount shopping experience with the exciting "blue light specials" during the day to push certain products for sale. The store was innovative, with products from clothing to hardware, including a deli and full restaurant all under one roof. Iva Mae had heard about and applied for a cooking position to work in the restaurant area, which became known as The Grill. She was hired as the assistant manager and began a new journey with the company.

Being the hard worker she had always been, Iva Mae did well with her new job and made friends easily. Even with working five days a week she was up early every morning to make breakfast for Bob, Robin, and Tammy. Her mornings would be rushed, taking care of the household while getting ready for work and then getting her children off to school. Since she had to be at work by eight o'clock, Robin and Tammy would be dropped at their school by seven thirty. They would walk home or get a ride from a friend, letting themselves into their house with their own key. At the end of the day, Iva Mae would be home by five thirty to cook dinner, take care of any laundry, and then, once all settled in for the evening, read the newspaper as her children controlled the television playing in the background. They seldom asked her to help with their homework, and when they did, she would tell them she didn't understand the "new" math. Her children had always done well in school, so she didn't concern herself about their education and grades.

Bob continued to find work locally with painting and wallpapering. He stayed out of Iva Mae's way and spent most of his time alone in the backyard with his transistor radio, listening to baseball games or other entertainment. He was proud of his work and bragged about it to those who would listen. He began to have his own friends who enjoyed fishing and other outdoor sports. He worked during the day and once home, became almost invisible.

Once Sandy had moved to St. Louis, Robin moved into her bedroom, and Tammy had the other bedroom to herself. Sandy and Iva Mae still had a close relationship. Sandy would make visits to Springfield, and she and Iva Mae would plan trips together. Iva Mae began traveling more during this time of her life. Her new job brought the most money she had been able to earn, and the financial benefits brought her a sense of freedom and some security.

The following year after Iva Mae had started working at Kmart, she got the bad news that her sister Lula had passed away suddenly. Lula was twenty years older than Iva Mae, but was only sixty-eight when she died. Roy, her husband, had passed away ten years earlier. Upon hearing the news, Iva Mae gathered her family and made the trip to Parsons, Kansas, to bury her sister and see what she could do for their family. She had always been close to Lula and counted on her for support. Lula had been a mother figure to Iva Mae, and she was saddened by the loss.

At this point in her life, Iva Mae was healthier than she had ever been. She had decided to go to Weight Watchers and began to lose weight. Sandy and Tammy both joined her on this weight loss journey. All were faithfully watching their portions and had tuna on everything they possibly could as part of the protein portion of their meals. The program was very structured then, and Iva Mae was very careful to buy just the right items so they would not have any room for error.

A couple of bumps in her health occurred during these years. One surgery ended in a hysterectomy followed by hormone shot treatments and later gallbladder surgery. Iva was losing much of the extra weight that she had carried most of her life. She felt good and was excited to be able to fit into dress sizes that she had never imagined wearing. Her love of clothes and shopping began, and she was proud of her accomplishments. She eventually reached her goal weight and became a lifetime member of Weight Watchers.

Miscellaneous family members would come and go with short stays and visits during these years on Main Street. Christmas was still a big holiday for the family and for Iva Mae. She would plan her gifts throughout the year, with many going into layaway on payment plans. Sometimes she would hide gifts that she had purchased so well that she would forget about them and find them after the holiday. For most years everyone would gather at Bob and Iva Mae's home for the gift giving and big dinner that had been under preparation over many days. Her children grew up knowing how important the Christmas holiday was to their mother and made trips home whenever possible.

Denny and Judy had their first son, Michael, in 1970 and moved to Washington, DC. Bob and Iva Mae actually made a trip to visit them together during the early seventies. It was a long drive and not exactly a good trip for them, because their relationship was just too broken to enjoy each other's company. Iva Mae had told Judy a few vague details about her relationship with Bob. She said, "Judy, I had no choice but to stay with him. I had four children to raise and no way of supporting them without him." Iva Mae lived in an era when women who were abused stayed in unhappy marriages because they felt they had no choice.

Bob was an outdoorsman and loved hunting, fishing, and enjoying nature. For years he would speak of the beauty of the mountains they had driven through on the trip. He enjoyed the scenery, but the trip was wearing for them both. Iva Mae had no interest in the outdoors or the beauty of the area, and wanted only to enjoy having her relatives together and being able to serve them big family meals and talk about her life. Iva Mae did talk about the sights that Denny took her to while in DC. She made her first trip to see the White House and the Capitol. She was so proud of her son and would tell anyone who would listen.

Bob and Iva Mae continued to take trips but not together. Bob took a trip to Denny and Judy's to work on renovations for their home. He enjoyed being able to help, but one of his treasured moments, which he often talked about, was the first and only professional baseball game he was able to see in person. He talked for years about seeing Hank Aaron hit one of his famous home runs.

Iva was increasing her friendships during these years. June was still her best friend, and they talked often if not daily on the phone. She began to do more with her coworkers at Kmart, including joining a bowling team. She faithfully went to church on Sunday morning and evening, with a trip to see her sister Mary in the country in between the services. Iva Mae seldom missed a Wednesday evening service as well, and she looked forward to the times the church had special speakers or revivals. She heard one such revival minister who preached on the Second Coming. Her curiosity was fired up, and she began to read the book of Revelation to learn more. The world was changing, and Iva Mae was convinced that her Lord was coming back for his faithful. The signs were there in the Bible, telling her that she should be ready.

During the early part of this decade, Robin began to move into her teenage years. She was becoming more involved with her church friends and interested in boys. Iva Mae was terrified that she would follow Sandy in the path of becoming an unwed mother. She could not bring herself to talk to Robin about sex or even how the reproductive system worked. She would say they needed to have a talk "someday" but never clarified what the talk would be about or why. She finally took Robin to a physician for an exam, and they left with a prescription for birth control pills. The pill had been available for only ten years, and surprisingly, Iva Mae didn't give it a second thought other than the comfort that it would prevent the embarrassment of having to deal with an unwed mother. At the time, her excuse, which was valid, was that Robin was having difficulty with her periods, which were very irregular, and the medication the doctor recommended would help.

As Robin started her high school years, she was having some problems. She didn't quite fit in and didn't enjoy school. Her grades were average, overall, because she didn't apply herself. She bored easily, didn't have close friends, and had very little confidence. She was not happy at home and felt torn between her mother and father. Robin's relationship with her father was close, and he shared his frustrations with her on occasion. She tried to become part of different groups at her school but never quite made more than a few connections or close friendships. She did not express her most secret feelings and wish for happiness and love.

Robin began to date in her early teens, but without any direction, she clumsily found a path to getting away from home and the tension that was always there. When she started a serious relationship with Bruce, a boy who was a few years older, Iva Mae let it happen since he and his family were part of her church. Bob was not happy about his little girl dating and did not like Bruce. He would leave the house whenever Bruce arrived and would not speak to him.

After about two years, Robin told her mom she wanted to get married. She was only sixteen, and Iva Mae agreed to let her, since she feared she would do it anyway by running away to Miami, Oklahoma, where she did not need permission. Seeing that as a scandal, she told Robin she would give her permission. Bob was not happy about the idea but was not asked or involved in the decision. Sandy was the only one who had a talk with Robin, trying to get her to understand what she was getting into and to think about how she was stepping into a new adult role. Robin was thinking only that this was a way out of a home that was in constant turmoil. The day the marriage took place in the pastor's office of the church, Robin's and Bruce's parents were the only attendees. It was the first time Robin had seen her father cry, and she just wanted to go home.

Once married, Robin was not doing very well. She was often sick and pretty lost in direction. Iva Mae came to her apartment once when she had the flu to take care of her. She cleaned up, made her food, and picked up some medicine. She was worried about Robin and later had her come back home so she could help her recover. Robin returned to her and Bruce's apartment after she began to feel better, but they were living separate lives. Neither spent much time there or together. Robin's marriage lasted less than a year, and then she divorced. She ended up moving in with a friend, Steve, with whom she worked at a pizza parlor. Iva Mae worried about her, but also told her that she had made her bed. She believed that Robin was grown up and on her own at that point. It wasn't long before Robin and Steve decided to plan a life together. They ended up getting married after Steve joined the Marine Corps and graduated from boot camp.

Iva and Sandy began to plan bigger trips together, the first of which was to go out West. They planned for Tammy and her best friend, Barbara, to go with them. Years later Tammy recalled that first road trip.

> Looking back, my first road trip with my family started a long history of disastrous road trips. Of course I did not know this at the time. The first trip when I was fourteen included my mother, sister, and best friend on a journey together to Yellowstone National Park. My twenty-six-year-old sister and my mother had planned this trip down to the day. They had gotten our first trip kit from a roadside assistance club that included some tour books. My sister Sandy lived in St. Louis, and the rest of the family lived in Springfield, Missouri. Mom and Sandy spent hours studying the maps and tour books, deciding where we would go on our trip. It was a happy time, and all winter we were all excited about our trip that coming August.

> We started out on August 20, in Mom's brand new 1975 Maverick. The four of us were on the road at last. Mom

had decided to start the trip at three o'clock in the morning, hoping that my best friend and I would sleep and not bother the adults. My best friend, Barbara, forgot to tell us that she had motion sickness, and her family forgot to tell us she had epilepsy even though we had known them for over a decade.

The first hint of trouble began when Barbara started throwing up. Now, I don't know if you have ever been trapped in a backseat with someone puking her guts out, but it isn't a pleasant place to be. The Maverick did not have a big backseat. We finally pulled over and stopped after I was covered in a very bad stench. At the gas station Barbara got some motion sickness pills and fell into a sleep coma. I was not so lucky; I was stuck in the backseat with the smell of vomit. Mom would not let us roll the windows down in the car, because it would blow her hair. Mother still had a 1960s hairstyle. It was kind of like a helmet that she sprayed hairspray on to make sure it never moved. She would go to the beauty parlor once a week, and then shellac it till the next week.

Our first night we stayed in Dodge City. Mom had read about it in the tour books. It was the first time I had seen Kansas. It was a dreary flatland with lots of dust. Dodge City was very cheesy to me. We went to a very cheap hotel, and Mom had brought food with us. So we had sandwiches and then went to a saloon show. It was supposed to convey a realistic picture of the old West. It didn't. The show was made up of college students in their summer jobs, dressed as saloon girls and gunslingers. They only served lemonade and sarsaparilla, both of which I really hated. There were all these kids whooping and hollering, and I just wanted to watch TV and go to bed. I just could not get into the "old West" spirit. We then walked around the area and looked at some cheap headstones that had epitaphs on them. They were not real either. Finally we got to the hotel and I went to sleep. To save money, Barbara and I slept in the same bed and my sister Sandy had the honor of sleeping with my mom. Because of Mom's hair, she had to sleep in one position with a special pillow that molded to her neck. That way her hair never touched the mattress.

The next morning we started the journey to the mountains at seven. Mom kept telling us that she was scared to drive in the mountains, and so she made Sandy promise to drive when we got there. As we got ready to roll, Sandy asked my mother what she would prefer, to get breakfast first, or to drive down the road awhile and get breakfast later. Sandy was trying to be considerate of my mother, because she was used to having a big breakfast. Mom said that she didn't care and that it was up to the rest of us. We took a vote, and since none of us were big breakfast eaters, we decided to wait.

We learned a very important lesson that day. Never believe my mother when she says she doesn't care. We pulled onto the highway, and after we arrived in the desolate Kansas flatlands, nowhere near a town, my mother started talking. I will never forget her refrain: "I am so hungry, and I just don't feel good unless I have my morning coffee." "You know, driving without anything to eat is making me feel faint." "I thought we were going to stop for breakfast." By then there was no place to stop. This went on until we found a restaurant and she got food. We practically pushed my mother into the restaurant. By then all we wanted was to shut her up. Mom got into the restaurant and could not understand why we all were in a pissy mood. We were all tired of my mother the martyr. After all of her griping, she just ordered toast and coffee. She said she wasn't that hungry. That was the start of another beautiful day on the road.

When we got back into the car, Barbara and I decided it was time to sing. You see, this was when you only had an AM radio in the car. Barbara and I started singing "Home on the Range." We sang it loudly and off-key. Sandy looked ready for Valium, but she hung in there. As the mountains started looming in front of us, my mother kept making Sandy promise to drive in the mountains. Mom said that it would make her too nervous to drive. We finally made it to Colorado Springs, where my mother had some cousins. We stayed the night at their house. It was an uneventful visit. Barbara and I got to watch TV and sleep on the floor.

The next day we started for Laramie, Wyoming. We made sure that Mom ate breakfast before we started on the road. We were in the mountains now, and so Sandy was doing all the driving. Barbara stayed awake, and she started to tell us stories of her love life. She was fifteen and had just broken up with her first boyfriend. We heard wonderful stories about how he had lured her into his room just so he could show her his sock drawer. He was a live wire. We laughed as we went down the road, and I had high hopes for the rest of the trip. That night we got to eat our evening meal in a restaurant for the first time. It upset my mother, and so she made us shop for groceries

before we left Laramie. Then we were on our way
to Yellowstone.

We had made reservations at Roosevelt Lodge in
Yellowstone. It had a main lodge and then cabins all
around. We had rented a cabin and started to settle into it.
The cabins were small, with two beds and a woodstove.
You had to walk a ways to the shower and bathrooms.
The people at the main lodge told us to watch out for
bears at night. My mother took it to heart and started
taking a log of wood with her back and forth to the
bathroom. She looked ridiculous carrying this stick
everywhere with her. Mom did not want to meet a bear.

One thing that we had overlooked was the cold. The
mountains get cold in August, and sometimes it snows.
My mother was cold. As you could probably guess, my
mother does not suffer in silence. So it began: "I am
freezing." "I am so cold." "I don't feel my feet." We
bought wood from the main lodge like there was a
shortage. We kept the cabin stove burning all the time. It
was so hot in the cabin that everyone wore summer
clothes, except my mother. My sister was kept busy
carting wood. The one thing my mother was happy about
was that she could cook on the woodstove. That way we
saved money and did not have to eat out.

Our first full day at Yellowstone was spent in the search
for long johns. All three of us were desperately searching
for long johns for my mother. We were all praying to find
a pair to shut her up. We drove all over Yellowstone, not
stopping to see the sights, not really caring at that
moment if we ever saw anything. We were focused on

long johns. We had a mission, and we went to every store in that park looking for any type of long johns. It was the quest we had been given. I don't know how many park stores we went to, but we found a pair at the store by the sulfur pits. Sandy bought them and then made my mother go straight to the bathroom there and put them on. We waited with bated breath to see if it shut her up. She came back to us content. We had completed the quest. By then it was in the evening, so we headed back to the cabin.

That evening I fell in love with Yellowstone. Barbara and I were dying to get away from my mother, and so we went to the main Roosevelt Lodge. There was a long porch in front of the lodge, and we sat in the chairs and watched the workers. What my mother did not know was that many college boys worked there. They were bored college boys. You see, there were no radio or television signals in the mountains. These boys worked, and when beer was shipped into the stores, they bought it all out.

Needless to say, there were not many girls working there. Barbara and I were the only new faces to be seen. As we sat in front of the lodge, boys started coming up to talk to us. We ended up with about twenty boys gathered around us. Barbara and I were in love with Yellowstone. My mother was not amused. She wanted us in the cabin after dark. She said she was scared of us running into bears or other wildlife—wildlife being the key word. It wasn't the bears she was afraid of, and my sister Sandy ran interference for us. I don't think we ever thanked her at the time. Sandy was not having a very good time. She was with my mother more than anyone should have had to be.

The next day we signed up for a horseback trip into the interior of the park. It was inaccessible by road. We met in front of the lodge and got our horses. Barbara got a horse that was so fat, her legs stuck out straight on the sides. I was told that I had a horse, but he looked like a white albino mule. It was the ugliest horse I had ever seen. Sandy had the pick of the litter. It looked like a normal horse. My mule was very bad tempered. He refused to go at any pace besides amble. He would stop to nip at anything, and sometimes that was other horses and riders. Everyone learned to stay away from us. We looked like a pair of lepers.

It was a peaceful day; my mother was not with us. While we were riding, we saw a moose with her calf. The guide told us to be quiet and stay away from them. My albino mule decided to charge them. I was along for the ride. The moose walked away with great dignity while my horse snorted and put on a show. I was bouncing everywhere but in the saddle. The guide rode up and got everything under control and gave me a lecture on obeying him. I told him it was not my problem but my mule's. We got back to the cabin, and all of us were saddle sore. I was walking straddle legged, and I know that I was a beautiful picture to watch. It is a sad statement on the loneliness of the boys there, for they still followed Barbara and me around.

It was that night that we found out that Barbara had epilepsy. I had known Barbara since I was two years old. I knew that she had funny fits sometimes, but I never knew what it was. Mom was cooking supper on the woodstove, and Barbara was talking to her. Then Barbara fell to the

floor and started having a grand mal seizure. Mom and
Sandy did not know what to think, and I stepped over
and put a spoon in her mouth to keep her from
swallowing her tongue.

Shit hit the fan. Barbara lived with her grandmother, who
was my mother's best friend. My mother was appalled
that she was never told about this, especially since she was
on a trip with us. It seemed that Barbara's family was
ashamed of her condition. I have never understood why.
This changed my mother for the rest of the trip. She
watched Barbara like she would drop and drool at any
minute. If she could have had her way, Barbara would
have been swathed in protective layers from anything
sharp from then on.

We had many more adventures that would take too long
to go into, but the highlight of the trip was on the fifth
day. We had been touring the different sections of the
park. Sandy had been driving us every day since Mom had
said over and over how she was afraid to drive in the
mountains. We started out that day to see Old Faithful.
My mother started complaining that morning that she was
not getting to drive her new car. She thought that Sandy
had taken it over. She was not happy that day. As we
drove to the geyser, Mom started complaining more and
more. We saw the geyser and went to a few other sights.
Sandy offered to let Mom drive, but Mom said, "I am
afraid to drive in the mountains." This went on all day.
Mom would complain, and Sandy would offer to let her
drive. Mom would say, "I told you that I am afraid to
drive up here."

Well, as we were driving back to our cabin, Mom complained just once too often. We were driving down the road, and there was a bear down the road on the opposite side of us. There were tourists pulled over trying to get a picture of the cute bear. These people are the kind that give Americans a bad name. You know, that stupid kind. These people were getting closer and closer to the bear, wanting that great photo. They had food out and were throwing it at the bear.

It was probably a potential disaster waiting to happen, but then we showed up. I have very seldom seen my sister lose her grip, but she had reached her limit. My mother was doing a repeat of her complaint of the driving issue for what seemed the hundredth time. Sandy pulled the car over to the side. She jumped out of the driver's side and went to the passenger side and pulled the car door open. She leaned over into my mother's face and said, "Get out and drive your own damn car." She didn't say it very loudly at first. Barbara and I were watching the tourist and bear show and trying to ignore what was going on in the front seat. Mother looked surprised, even shocked, that Sandy was asking her to drive. She didn't realize that she had been rubbing on Sandy's last raw nerve for days. Mom answered in a quiet voice, "I have told you and told you that I am afraid to drive in the mountains." Sandy looked ready to do bodily harm and said, "You have been bitching about me driving the car for days, that it is your new car and you are not getting to drive it."

Barbara and I were now dividing our attention between the bear and the conflict beside us. Sandy began to get louder as she insisted that Mother drive. Mom was getting louder in her refusal. The tourists were beginning to watch us instead of the bear. I knew that Sandy was determined that my mother was going to drive. It was getting louder and louder on our side of the road. I knew it had gotten out of hand when the bear stopped paying attention to the tourists and the food to watch our conflict.

Barbara and I had a choice at that time. We could try to hide in the floorboard from the tourists, or we could add to the chaos. We went for chaos. We started singing our rendition of "Home on the Range." Sandy and Mother were trying to argue above us, the bear got scared and ran off, and the tourists gawked at these people from the Show Me state. Mother drove for the next three days.

It was after this trip that Iva Mae became sick with a cold. That cold was the beginning of an illness that was many years later discovered to be bronchiectasis, a condition in which her bronchial tubes were permanently damaged and enlarged, allowing bacteria and mucus to build up. It was never discovered what had caused the disease, but the trip west and illness had brought it to the surface. This incurable lung disease gave her a chronic cough and shortness of breath, and had her living on antibiotics more often than not for the rest of her life.

Iva Mae preparing a holiday dinner

Chapter 29

The 1970s were a volatile decade, with many changes in lifestyle, clothing, and spending. By the middle of the decade the Vietnam War had ended, inflation was rising faster than ever, a president had resigned in disgrace, and many groups were still fighting for equality. By 1976 technology had brought the first laser printer, and NASA introduced the space shuttle Enterprise.

At age fifty-four, Iva Mae had been with Kmart going on seven years. Her circle of friends had continued to enlarge, and she still went to church as often but mostly by herself. Sixteen-year-old Tammy was still at home, but between school, friends, and odd jobs, she was gone a lot.

Iva Mae and Tammy's relationship was explosive at best. Tammy was the most demanding of her children and always had been, and Iva Mae mostly gave in to her. Over the years it was speculated that Iva Mae felt guilty because of Tammy's birth defect. As Tammy was growing up, Iva Mae accused her of being just like her father. She said she had his temper and family traits, but in reality she was much like her mother.

Bob at age sixty-six was still working jobs that he found mainly through word of mouth. He began to suffer from poor circulation, and his legs often bothered him. Bob was proud of his work. He had become an accomplished painter and wallpaper hanger with an excellent reputation in the area. He would proudly talk about the commercial jobs he had completed and show them off with details about the types of materials and techniques he had used. He was often gone, spending time with friends who enjoyed the same conversations about hunting and fishing or talking about the craftsman work they did.

The holiday season of 1976 was special for Iva Mae because all her children were coming home for Christmas. She had been planning and preparing for the gift giving and, even more important, the meals for weeks.

> One Christmas on Main Street in Springfield everyone came home for the holiday, including all the dogs. I was working at Kmart, and at Christmas you were so busy. So I would work all day, and then I had to make candy, bread, and cookies at night, but I always got everything done. I would make chocolate chip cookies, sugar cookies that would be in the shapes of Christmas trees, bells, and stars. These cookies would have sugar icing on them in

Christmas colors. I made chocolate fudge, peanut butter fudge, peanut brittle, and divinity fudge. Then I would begin on the homemade breads, hot rolls, cakes, pies, and a few other new recipes that I would find each year.

I usually fixed a huge dinner with turkey and ham for Christmas dinner, so I would plan on many of the same side dishes but a few new ones too. I always made dressing, and mashed potatoes with gravy as well as corn. Then I would have ambrosia salad and another Jell-O salad with fruit. Of course we always had cranberry salad and green bean casserole. My sister Mary was the pie maker, and she would always bring three different pies for the dinner.

This year we had our Christmas tree up, and then they "blue lighted," which means real cheap, trees at Kmart, and I brought one home. Tammy and Barbara, Tammy's best friend, took the old tree down and put the new one up. Barbara always spent Christmas with us. She would open her presents at home, then call to see if she could come over to our house.

This Christmas was very special because all my children came home: Denny and Judy with their sons, Mike and Brian, from Washington, DC; Sandy and her sheepdog mix, Ralph, from St. Louis; and Robin and Steve and their Doberman, Dax. Steve was to leave right after Christmas for Okinawa, which made Robin very sad.

The tree was set up in the living room in front of the picture window that faced the street. We had presents all over the floor, and Brian was about a year and half old. He loved playing with the presents. He wouldn't open them, just pick them up and look at them. While I was at work, Denny bought me a new color television as a Christmas present. We had never had a color television. This was our first. No one told me about buying it, and they installed it in the same place as the black-and-white TV and got rid of the old one. When I came home, they turned the television on, and I didn't notice it was in color for some time, and they really teased me because I didn't notice.

Denny and Judy were staying at Judy's parents' home, and Mike and Brian were staying with us. I had several days off, and having them kept me busy. The house was full with everyone, but we managed to fit everyone in, even the dogs.

We opened the gifts early on Christmas morning, and that took some time since there were so many of us and so many gifts. Then we had my homemade cinnamon rolls, coffee, and hot chocolate. Right after breakfast I started to work on our Christmas dinner. My sister Mary and her family always came to have Christmas dinner with us. They would arrive, and Mary and I would visit while working in the kitchen. I would always buy bags of different types of nuts and have them in bowls around the house for everyone to crack their own to snack on along with all the cookies and candy. The kids would all be playing with their gifts and moving everything out of the living room. Barbara would be calling to see if she could come over to have dinner with us. The television would be playing while everyone watched or napped, waiting for dinner.

That afternoon while we were visiting, we put the dogs in our bedroom, and you guessed it, they got into my yarn, and did they make a mess.

Everyone stayed several days, so we really had fun. It was really crowded at the house, especially since we had only one bathroom. Everyone just had to take a turn. After everyone left, I was ready to go back to work and rest up.

Iva Mae was very angry with Bob that Christmas. Denny had gotten Bob a bottle of liquor, and on Christmas morning, the two of them disappeared for a few hours. Iva Mae was furious with Bob because everything had to wait for their return so dinner could be served. Of course, she blamed only Bob, not Denny. She never found fault with her son even if she didn't agree with his decisions. Iva Mae had a way of looking at life and finding a justification for her decisions. Her moral compass was the Bible, or at least the way she understood it. She had regrets, but would say she had no choices. Her greatest strength— and her greatest weakness—was her ability to not question her past decisions. When Iva Mae looked back on her past, it was to point out the mistakes others had made, not to look at her own decisions. After all, her decisions couldn't be questioned, because she'd had no choice.

After the holiday, Denny's family went back to Washington, DC. Tammy and Sandy left for a trip to New Orleans on an adventure together. Steve left for his tour overseas, and Robin was going back and forth between her parents' home and her in-laws' home just south of Kansas City for the next year. During that year Robin and Iva Mae spent a lot of time together, shopping and going out to eat, and they became better friends, enjoying each other's company for the most part. The situation at home was still very uncomfortable, as Iva Mae had no tolerance for Bob at all, and that put Robin in the middle of them much of the time. A year later Robin moved on to the next military station with Steve once he had returned to the United States. Iva Mae had become more independent, and her circle of friends between church and work had grown, which kept her busy.

Chapter 30

y the late 1970s Iva Mae was ready to make her next move. She had been thinking about her life for some time and had decided that once Tammy was through high school, she was going to divorce Bob and be on her own. She had said many years earlier, "I had no choice but to stay with him. I had four children to raise and no way of supporting them without him." Tammy was at the end of her high school years, so the opportunity had arrived. Tammy had spent part of her high school years in St. Louis living with Sandy. Tammy and Iva Mae's relationship had become more difficult through the years, and Sandy had stepped in to provide an outlet for them both.

Tammy had completed high school early and would be graduating at almost seventeen. She really had no direction and was looking to party with friends and explore life. Her grades were above average, but although she received several scholarship offers, she was not mature enough to see the value of college or ready to pursue it. Iva Mae did not like her friends, and Tammy had no interest in the church or the friends her mother would have preferred. Their relationship was volatile at best, with Iva Mae reminding Tammy how much she was like her father and believing something was wrong with her. She had had Tammy in therapy several years earlier when she was in her early teens and confronted with fines from the library. Tammy was an avid reader much like her mother had been at her age.

Tammy had an unusual view on life and marched to a different drummer. She became more eclectic as she aged. Her love of reading began at an early age, as she wrote later in life:

> I love to read and it is my addiction. I have been reading books since second grade. I started out reading the Nancy Drew mysteries. My second-grade teacher read one aloud to us, and I was hooked. I tried to get my mother to read to me, but she ironed for people, babysat four other children, and ran a household for a family of kids that had a seventeen-year age span. She just did not have the spare time to read to me. I have been reading books ever since. When I was a child, I would ask any adult about a word I

didn't understand. I would stop any adult to ask, as I wanted to know everything about what I was reading. I loved to get a new book and tear into the story.

My family encouraged me to read, as it kept me quiet. I would sit for hours wrapped up in a story. I started out with the Nancy Drew books, and then went on to great adventures. I loved Walter Farley's Black Stallion books, Laura Ingalls Wilder's Little House series, and Louisa May Alcott's Little Women series. I would get wrapped up in the books where the world could be falling in around me and I would not notice.

My family had quite a few arguments, as everyone was strong-minded, and I could tune out everyone with a book. People did not understand how wrapped up I could get in written pages. When you read a good book, you become involved in the story. You feel that you are there, living it with the characters. A good book fills your mind, and you can see what is happening. Often you can feel what the characters are feeling. When I was in second and third grade, I read *Little Women* over and over. Every time the character Beth died, I cried. It didn't matter how many times I read the book, I always cried.

I wasn't a child that was athletic, and I had no coordination. I was never picked for sports, and I didn't have much competition in me. I would rather be reading. I had teachers take away my books at recess time. I would rather read than play kickball or any games. I had my books taken away by teachers that wanted me to participate in class. I would do my class work as quickly as possible so that I could get back to my book.

My sister Robin was not happy with my love of reading. We had played dress-up, make-believe, and board games before my addiction. We were to clean the house on Saturdays for my mother. Robin would get very irritated with me because I would read all day. I would go to the store to get comic books and candy for us both, and then retire to my room to read. Robin would want to get the housework done before my mother came home. I would usually end up in the one room with a door lock. I would be sitting on the bathroom floor with my book while Robin banged on the door threatening to call Mom.

During the summer breaks I would get to go to the library once a week. I would take two people with me to carry the books out. I would average twenty-five to thirty books a week. I would read my summer away. I was captivated by the stories of *Quo Vadis*, *Les Miserables*, and *Lord of the Rings*. While other kids were bored, I was having adventures all over this world and in other worlds that authors made up. I would read anything. I would read the cereal boxes at breakfast.

My parents became worried that I did not get enough exercise or sun, and so I was forced to ride my bike every night. I would take my book with me and read as I rode my bike. One night I ran into a parked car in front of my house. I flew over the handlebars and landed on the parked car's trunk. I still had my book in my hands though. Unfortunately my parents witnessed the whole episode. After that I was patted down for books before I was sent to my bike. Everyone in our neighborhood knew of my love of reading. I would not go anywhere without a book.

Tammy actually found a way to block out the constant tension of her home life by disappearing into the world of books. Unfortunately she didn't realize that she had formed a nervous habit of tearing the corners of the books and chewing on them while reading. The library took notice and notified Iva Mae, who panicked, fearing that she was going to have to pay for all the damage to the books. Although she did not really agree with the idea of taking Tammy to a psychologist as a physician recommended, she scheduled an appointment. The psychologist had a couple of meetings with Tammy and told Iva Mae that he would like to meet with her as well. Iva Mae took offense: she knew there was nothing wrong with her. Tammy was the one with the issue. Tammy had a few more meetings alone, until Iva Mae decided that it was not helping and ended the appointments. Once Tammy had become aware of what she was doing with the books, she quit and found other ways of working out her nervous tension.

As Tammy reached the end of her school years, Iva Mae told Bob she wanted a divorce. Bob didn't fight her. He was resigned to Iva Mae getting her way. He was tired, and at sixty-eight, his health was showing signs of wear. Tammy's thoughts best summed up Bob's life:

> My father seemed always busy. He was a fisherman and a hunter. He painted houses, hung vinyl, and did whatever he could to bring home money. Dad seemed to travel often to find work. When I was small, I remember him getting us kids out of the backyard trees where we would play and make up games.
>
> The clearest memory of my father is when I saw him play baseball one time. He seemed so strong and athletic. I

thought he could hit and throw the ball better than anyone in the world.

The other times spent with my dad were during storms. He loved to sit outside and watch a storm roll in. My sister Robin and I would sit in the front porch swing and watch the weather with him. He was a very quiet man at home. Our home was definitely a matriarchy. My mother was the boss, and woe to the person who didn't realize it. Looking back, it seems that my father got more distant every year.

My parents did not get along, and it got worse every year of their marriage. They finally got a divorce when I was sixteen, and I believe everyone in the family was relieved. Watching such a terrible marriage affected everyone in the family. To this day I never want to get married.

Chapter 31

The divorce was fairly easy, as Iva Mae decided that Bob could have everything she didn't want; whatever neither of them took went into a garage sale. Even then they divided the profit by what was sold of his and hers. Once the house was sold, Iva Mae moved herself and Tammy into an apartment with Sandy's help. Bob moved into a small house in Springfield that Denny had purchased and rented out. Iva Mae was happy to be done with Bob and everything involved with putting up with him. She had even received a letter from Bob's son telling her he did not blame her for the split, as he knew that Bob was a difficult person.

Iva Mae was excited about having her own place, but once again she didn't feel financially secure since she knew that everything was dependent on her. She was coming up on ten years of working with Kmart, and at fifty-six years old, she was tired. She had continued to enlarge her circle of friends, and now that she was able, would plan trips with them. Tammy was a worry, because she was in a group of friends of whom Iva Mae did not approve. They did not get along well at all, and Tammy avoided her if at all possible.

It was 1978 and the oil crisis was over, but the results were Japanese car imports accounting for half the United States import market. The newest craze was a computer video game called Space Invaders. The "Son of Sam" was convicted of murder in New York, and the movies *Grease*, *Saturday Night Fever*, and *Close Encounters of the Third Kind* changed the pop culture of the world.

Iva Mae started to travel with a group of women who were her closest friends. She enjoyed their company and loved the attention they gave her. She felt confident with them and was able to laugh a lot about life in general. At the same time she wanted more security. All her life she had been looking for a safe place where she would not have to worry about money, but she just never seemed to feel that safety.

One of her trips during this period was with Sandy. The two of them drove in Sandy's car to Washington, DC, to visit Denny and Judy. The plan was to pick up their children, Mike and Brian, and go to Florida for a fun-filled vacation to Disney

World, SeaWorld, and Marineland. On the way, they stopped in Cherry Point, North Carolina, to pick up Robin, who had been living on the military base with Steve since his return from overseas. She just happened to be off from work during that week, so she could join in on the trip.

Denny and Judy's children were the perfect age for a Disney World trip. Brian was just turning three, and Mike was eight. Iva Mae was shocked to find out after they were on the road that Brian had packed his own suitcase and brought one change of clothes for the entire trip. It was the subject of discussion during that summer's trip as well as for many years afterward. The idea of letting a three-year-old pack his own suitcase for an extended trip was unbelievable to Iva Mae, and she found it irritating as well as an inconvenience. The group went on a shopping expedition to pick up extra clothing, and were then on their way to the state of magic, dreams, and fun.

The trip was a typical Iva Mae journey. All was fine as long as the schedule was kept and she was comfortable. The trip between North Carolina and Orlando was uneventful other than the stops for gas and food. Mike, as the older of the two boys, was smart and knew how to get Brian to agree with what he wanted to do or how to manipulate the group to get his way often. As brothers, they got along and traveled well. This was the first long trip Robin had taken with Sandy or her mother in many years. Although she had spent time with Sandy in the past, visiting her in St. Louis and going on a couple of camping trips with her, Tammy, and Iva Mae, this was the first trip they became real friends. Each evening after dinner and a swim in the motel pool, Iva Mae went to bed with the children, and Robin and Sandy would spend time together talking outside and enjoying the Florida weather.

Sandy told Robin stories about her life that Robin had never heard. Robin heard about childhood memories and about Sandy's current life, friends, and lovers. And although Robin had found old letters in the attic years later that were written during Sandy's months in the unwed mothers' home, she didn't really know what had happened until Sandy told her on that trip to Florida. Sandy felt great resentment toward her mother about the baby she had been forced to give up. She also shared her feelings about Bob and how he had treated her during that time. She told Robin that if Bob was dying of thirst on her front porch, she would not give him a drink.

Her anger was just below the surface, and talking about it on that trip, coupled with Iva Mae's insistence on getting everything she wanted and needed, brought it out more. Each morning Iva Mae would start the day by telling Sandy that she needed coffee and breakfast. Sandy would ask her what she wanted to eat, and Iva Mae would tell her she didn't know. Once Sandy had picked the place and everyone was seated, Iva Mae would tell her she would have preferred something else. During the entire trip, there were numerous conversations about food, the place to stay for the evening, and anything else about which a decision needed to be made.

Overall, though, the week on the road went quickly and was fun. The time spent at Disney World was special for them all. Because the park had been open for only seven years, it was still small and everything felt new and modern. The Magic Kingdom, along with a few resorts, made up the entire park during this time. Sandy and Iva Mae chose a motel outside the park, and although the group's day in the Magic Kingdom was special, it was also very tiring. It was the end of June, and the park was busy. Arriving early at the opening and staying until the fireworks at the end made for a full day.

The following day was a full one at a different park, SeaWorld, which had opened in 1973. It was a hot summer day, and Iva Mae complained about it often. She did not like being uncomfortable, and once she decided she was not happy, everyone would know she was unhappy even if it could not be changed. It was almost as if she wanted the people around her to feel just as miserable as she did. The highlight of the day was during the Shamu killer whale show when everyone was completely doused with water from a giant splash. Iva Mae was worried about her hair, as she still had a "helmet head" hairstyle that was carefully kept a week at a time, but even she was in better spirits after being cooled off by the water.

After the park visits in Orlando, the group drove to the eastern coast, with a stop at Cape Canaveral. It was an exciting time to visit since the space shuttle was in the process of being built and the displays of the moon landing could be seen close up in a room to depict how it would have looked. Everyone enjoyed the displays and information, including the tour to the tower where the space shuttle was being assembled. But the trip was getting long at this point, and everyone was showing signs of wear.

The following day they drove to Marineland. Sandy was becoming increasingly irritated with her mother by now, as nothing seemed to please her or be at her convenience. Sandy's feelings about the past had been growing throughout the trip, and Iva Mae's complaints and self-centered needs were sending her over the edge of patience. Even Mike and Brian seemed to feel the pressure building and kept on the side of good behavior. Robin was pretty much a sounding board for both

Sandy and Iva Mae, and in usual fashion she was able to
not think about it too much and compartmentalize the
mounting stress.

A better multistory motel on the beach was the stop for the
evening. They all enjoyed the late afternoon into dusk on the
beach and playing on the edge of the water. Unfortunately the
mosquito population was in full force and they were
unprepared for the onslaught of bites, so everyone went back
to the room slapping and scratching. The Marineland show
was an entertaining afternoon the next day, but the facility was
on a downhill slide after many successful years. The opening of
SeaWorld was changing the kind of entertainment audiences
were looking for in the Florida world of fun.

After the show, it was a drive up the coast to the historic city
of St. Augustine. Sandy had been looking forward to seeing the
city and learning more about its history, but Iva Mae was tired
and did not want to stop. She was ready for the trip to be over
and wanted to get back to Robin's house before continuing on
to Washington, DC. Sandy's temper was on edge, but she
didn't feel like arguing, so they drove through and continued
on. That evening Sandy told Robin she had had enough and
was done. Robin wasn't sure what that meant at the moment
but knew that it was not going to be good.

Once the group arrived back at Robin and Steve's home on the
base in North Carolina, Sandy told her mother how she felt.
All the pain she had been carrying over the years came out like
a volcanic eruption. The years of responsibility instead of a
childhood, being abandoned, giving up her baby—it all spewed
out. Iva Mae was in total shock. She didn't understand why
Sandy was so angry. Didn't she know that she had done her

best under the circumstances? Sandy told her that she was going back home by herself and that she would arrange and pay for Iva Mae and the children to fly back. She had had enough, packed her bags, and left. Robin had to deal with the aftermath of her mother's questions, justifications, and tears.

Sandy and Iva Mae did make up sometime afterward and spent many years going places together. But for the rest of their days, Iva Mae knew not to push Sandy too far.

ROBIN ANNE GRIFFITHS

Chapter 32

Iva Mae had moved herself and Tammy into an apartment after her divorce. Tammy was an unhappy, rebellious teenager, and Iva Mae constantly compared her to her father, pointing out the qualities that she thought were bad ones. She had been at Kmart for ten years and was tired and looking for support and security. All her life she worried about being safe. Her greatest fears were not having money or a place to live. About this same time Denny and Judy needed help with their two boys in Washington, DC. Through conversations with Iva Mae it was decided that she would move to Washington and live with them to help take care of the boys while they were busy in their careers. Iva Mae was excited about this new adventure and the thought that she would have more security and safety in her life. She and Sandy found an apartment for Tammy and moved her in, even though Tammy, working or not, wasn't really prepared to be on her own.

Not long after Iva Mae moved, Tammy was in trouble. She seemed unable to handle her life and found herself without enough money and in a lot of debt. Robin and Steve had moved to Kansas City after Steve was discharged from the service and offered to have Tammy come live with them so she could get back on her feet.

Iva Mae had a new and different world to learn after moving to Washington, DC. Denny worked in the District for the Veterans Administration, and Judy was the warden in a Virginia prison. They had a home in Bethesda, Maryland, where Iva Mae had the lower part of the house to herself with a large bedroom and bathroom. She had many adjustments to go through as she began her new life in the capital. Driving was one of the many adjustments, as she found her way to schools, sporting events, shopping, and other entertainment around the area. She also learned the subway system and easily began new friendships with the parents of Brian and Michael's friends. Iva Mae's faith in God guided her to a new church and more new friendships. This was the first time she was exposed to many diverse relationships and new thoughts that were far from her upbringing in Kansas and the Bible Belt of Missouri.

While living in Maryland, Iva Mae had many of her friends visit her from Missouri and enjoyed showing them around the city. She especially enjoyed taking them to the White House on the tour and once had a special visit that included lunch and the famous bean soup in the United States Senate dining room. Iva Mae then was able to attend the hearing when Denny was nominated by President Jimmy Carter to be deputy assistant secretary for veterans' employment. It was one of her proudest moments as a mother. She was settling into her new life and loved the attention she received as the mother of a well-known and respected son. Iva Mae was learning a new lifestyle and started walking and getting more exercise. She enjoyed the responsibility she had with her grandchildren and felt secure in her life.

In 1980, while Iva Mae was living in Washington, her sister Mary died. At eighty years old she had been suffering from Alzheimer's disease. Iva Mae worried that she would suffer the same fate and asked Sandy and Robin to watch for signs so she would know if she had the disease. Mary's death did not affect her as much as Lula's, but the circumstances of Mary's aging and the failures she was suffering made her passing more of a blessing.

Iva Mae began a life of adventure when she moved to Washington, DC. The summer after she moved there, the family set out for a trip to Hawaii. This was exciting, as she was exposed to and experienced many new and different people and ways of life. Hawaii was beautiful, and she was thrilled to be able to see so much of it in a short span of time. Her favorite story from that trip was when she went out from the beach on a catamaran with the boys. She was on the back of the boat with a large group of people. This definitely took her out of her comfort zone, because Iva Mae had never learned to swim and was not comfortable on the water. But she never passed up a chance to experience something new, even if it included a wild ride on the water, getting splashed and wet, and thinking she was going to fall out of the boat.

She shopped, and on the way back from their trip, they stopped in San Francisco, where she experienced a different type of adventure as the hotel workers were having a strike. Iva Mae had always loved to watch people, and she spent much of one evening watching the people on the street as they marched. It was her favorite story to tell of being in San Francisco.

Other trips followed for Iva Mae. She enjoyed family trips to New York, where she saw the Macy's Thanksgiving Day parade and the Rockettes' Christmas show at Radio City Music Hall. She was in awe of the size of New York City and years later still talked about Radio City Music Hall and how it was such a wonderful show. On another trip she visited Niagara Falls and took the *Maid of the Mist* boat tour. Each trip was an adventure to Iva Mae, and she kept memories of them to talk about for years.

The following Christmas she returned to Missouri to visit with Sandy and Robin and help with another move for Tammy.

Steve and Robin were living in Kansas City, and Tammy was living with them. Steve was working for the railroad. He had got out of the marines but was getting ready to go to Saudi Arabia with a new job. I was living up at Washington, DC, and Sandy was living in St. Louis. So I came down on the plane and went to Kansas City with Sandy. She had a van and was going to move Tammy back to her home.

Steve and Robin were renting a small house and only had one bathroom, so we all had to take turns getting ready for anything we were doing.

We opened our presents on Christmas Eve and we started a new way of celebrating gift giving. We handed out one present at a time and that person opened his present and everyone knew what they got. It takes forever but it is fun. We still do that every Christmas to this day. I had been to Hawaii that summer with Denny and his family and got muumuu dresses for the girls.

The next day Steve's folks and his brother and girlfriend came, and we fixed a big Christmas dinner. Robin had heart failure when her oven wouldn't work at first, but we made it work. The next day we had to load Tammy's things up and go back to St. Louis and me back to Washington, DC.

ROBIN ANNE GRIFFITHS

Chapter 33

Iva Mae's style was changing during her life in Washington. Her taste in clothes became more selective, and her idea of fun shopping was to go to stores like Lord and Taylor even to window-shop. She had come a long way from the days of having hardly enough money to buy underwear. Eating at different restaurants and shopping were becoming her favorite outings. She enjoyed going out with new friends to church concerts and lunches as well as spending time talking to her old friends from Springfield about her new life.

But times were changing for her son. Denny and Judy made the decision to separate and then divorce. Denny had moved out of their home, and Mike and Brian as well as Iva Mae stayed with Judy. Iva Mae found humor in the situation and for many years told people that her daughter-in-law got custody of her in the divorce settlement. Although she tried to make light of it to others, she was shaken by the change. She did not like Judy's new lifestyle of dating and disagreed with her way of raising children. She thought the boys were in trouble. She worried about Brian, but was more concerned about Mike, who was running the streets.

The following year Iva Mae found she wanted to take care of herself a little more. Living in the Washington area required more walking than other places she had lived, so she started walking for exercise.

It was a dreary Saturday in Bethesda, Maryland. It wasn't cold for February but had drizzled and been cloudy all day till that afternoon and the sun came out and looked so pretty. I was by myself, as everyone had gone to do their own thing, so I decided to take a health walk. Maybe it would cheer me up. I started down Governor Street and it really felt good. I decided to turn at Governor School and go down by the school. I had never walked down that way before. After I had gone about a block, I slipped on a wet leaf and down I went, flat on my leg. It wasn't a bad fall and I looked around to see if anyone had seen me. There was no one around so I got up, but did my ankle hurt. It was really painful. I brushed the mud off of my coat and pants and decided I had better go home.

Well, I started walking and I had six blocks to go before I could get home. My ankle hurt more and more and I was wondering if I could make it, but I did. Next step to take was to go to the emergency room, so I changed my pants and wiped the mud off my shoes. Then I climbed into my yellow 1978 Pinto car and drove myself to the Bethesda Naval Hospital, which was about two and a half miles from where we lived.

By this time my ankle was swelling and turning blue. The doctor finally got around to me and looked it over and punched around on it and said, "Do you think it needs an X-ray?" It was really hurting and something was wrong. I told the doctor that I didn't think it would hurt. After so long a time they X-rayed my ankle and the doctor brought me the results. The doctor said, "Well, do you want me to eat my hat now or later?" It was broken and he said if I had waited till morning, I would have had to have surgery. They put the cast on me and the cast was from my ankle to my hip on the right leg. There was no way I could drive home. I hadn't been on crutches in my life, and I was big and awkward and that didn't help me at all. They tried to teach me how to use the crutches, but I wasn't a good pupil.

They called home and Judy, my daughter-in-law, was home, so she came after me. The attendants helped me into the front seat, but I couldn't get my leg in. Thank goodness it was a four-door car. So I had to get out and then try to get in the backseat. It was an effort with help. It would have been funny but it hurt too badly. Then I thought, *How am I going to get in the house? If I go in the front door, there are steps and more steps down to my room.* There was a door around at the side of the house with no steps, but it would be lots of walking on partly frozen ground. Judy is small so she would be no help. We decided to stop at some friends' house and see if Greg would help me. They were having a party and Greg had had several before-dinner drinks, but he stopped everything and came to assist.

Greg was really feeling good and quite funny, so they got me out of the car and we started for the door. It was so hard to walk on the grass that was partly frozen, and I was not doing very good on crutches. I also had to go to the bathroom so bad that I thought I was going to wet my pants. Greg was trying to help me too much, and he was being very funny. I told him he had better stop or I probably would use the bathroom right there. I finally got in the house and to the bed, and they left me and went after my car.

I still hadn't been to the bathroom. I laid there awhile and finally got myself up and proceeded to the bathroom, which seemed a long journey but really wasn't. I made it to the bathroom and back to the bed. Then I took another pain pill. Tomorrow will be another day.

At that point Iva Mae was overweight and not in the best of shape. She still suffered from hypertension, phlebitis, and other small ailments, so using crutches was difficult at best. Living in a two-story home made getting to the upstairs kitchen impossible, so she counted on Mike and Brian to help her get food. The boys, as young as they were, took their job of caring for their grandmother seriously and brought her a variety of peanut butter sandwiches and other items that, although not the best choice for her, did the job of satisfying hunger.

In later years Brian told this story about his grandmother living with them:

> Thinking of stories is tough, considering I was so young when she raised me. The only ones I can remember is she swears up and down one time she went to the park with Mike and made more baskets than him (basketball). She feels God must have done something, because she'd just say, "I remember making more baskets than Mike that day" over and over. She was really proud and repeated this story often.
>
> Also, I kind of remember her breaking her leg but still walking about a mile home since no one was around to help—pretty amazing. Finally, she used to always say *the devil himself* had created our round dining room table since that is the way I could keep away from her when she was trying to catch me. I'd just run in circles, and it really drove her crazy.

Mike, being a little older during these years, later wrote these memories:

> It seems just like yesterday that I was a student in the first grade preparing to have my customary lunch sandwich of peanut butter and jelly on white bread. My undeveloped yet sophisticated taste buds would be satisfied with nothing less than perfection. Today, however, there was cause for worry. Rather than the usual sandwich maker, my grandma Hodge would be taking over the reins. She had recently come to live with my family at our house in suburban Maryland. Her references in regard to cooking

were exemplary, I'll admit. Both of my parents had raved to me about her prowess in creating culinary treats. I would take a lot of convincing though.

So it was with great trepidation that day that I opened my Evel Knievel lunchbox. A wave of relief swept over me as I surveyed the usual contents: a peanut butter and jelly sandwich, a bag of Fritos, and an apple. I unwrapped the sandwich, sank my teeth into the soft and fluffy bread, and was ready to float off into peanut butter and jelly nirvana when to my horror, my utter horror, there was butter—yellow repulsive butter—spread all over the bread of my peanut butter, butter, and jelly sandwich. Needless to say, I was unable to finish my meal that fateful day. Would I faint from lack of nutrition? How many brain cells would perish? How would I make it through the day?

Conjuring the strength of the ages, I made it through that day. I don't know how, and the lesson plans are still a bit foggy, but I did. In my weakened state, I returned home and confronted my grandmother about this cruel hoax. By her response, I don't think she realized the enormity of what I had been through. She replied that most people in the Ozarks had butter with their peanut butter and jelly, but that she'd be happy to leave it off the next day. Then she asked if there was anything she could make me. Well, she couldn't cook, but at least she seemed nice.

As I got older and my tastes developed, her cooking improved noticeably. Now, don't get me wrong. There were exceptions, such as the mayonnaise incident on my ham and cheese in third grade. But time heals all wounds, and it was all uphill from there. How many delicious meals I enjoyed being served from her kitchen I do not know, but there were many. The fried chicken, expertly battered and well-seasoned, fried to a crisp golden brown and accompanied with mashed potatoes of the perfect consistency. The succulent pork chop with a side of applesauce and buttered corn on the cob or the chicken-fried steak with a gravy that could not hope to be duplicated by the most master of chefs. Yet the crème de la crème, the piece de resistance: her chocolate chip cookies. It was as if my prayers had been answered. To bite into one right as it was coming out of the oven. It was heavenly. *Très magnifique!*

Shortly afterward, roughly fourth grade, as I was devising a plan to open Grandma Hodge's Chocolate Chip Cookies shops around the nation, the unthinkable happened: Grandma broke her leg. She returned from the hospital in a cast and was helped into her bed. I was informed that with my parents off at work, my little brother and I would be responsible for preparing her daily lunch. Finally, it was my chance to repay Grandma a small bit for all the wonderful meals that she had made for me. I crafted one of my specialties for her first lunch: a ham and cheese sandwich, superbly made, alongside a bag of potato chips and a Dr. Pepper. I brought it to her room as if it were a grand feast and placed it elegantly next to the bedside. She woke up from a deep sleep, eventually ate her lunch, and thanked me for a meal well done. Then, she asked if tomorrow she could have her lunch closer to noon, instead of eight o'clock in the morning, which was the present time.

Like so many things in life, you don't really appreciate people and the things they do until they're no longer there. It first happened when I went to a friend's house for dinner of improperly fried chicken and lumpy mashed potatoes. There were many others as well. But I let the world know about my grandmother's cooking powers and told them how incredible her chocolate chip cookies are. To my disbelief, there were some who replied that their grandmother's cookies were great as well. No, no, no, no, no, no, my grandmother's cookies really ARE the best. To prove my point I did a scientific experiment with the gang at school by which my grandmother's cookies were placed aside the competitor's and needless to say, mine won hands down. Unfortunately, it was a self-defeating experiment because I was now short several cookies. But others would follow.

Clearly I enjoyed her cooking, but even more so talking over dinner, hearing the family stories. Like how funny it was when my dad introduced his new girlfriend to her (my future mom), and they were completely drunk from a moonshine called Purple Cow. Even watching soap operas during the summer like *Days of Our Lives*—my intricate knowledge of the old Bo's and Roman's compared to the new ones would assist me later in life in making my own female acquaintances. But, most valuable to me is the time I got to spend with her enriching my childhood, and for that (and the cookies) I will be eternally grateful.

After Iva Mae broke her ankle, Robin came the following March to visit and stay with her to help with her care. Iva Mae was grateful, as television and the meals she was getting from her grandchildren were getting boring, and she was looking forward to the company. Robin was preparing to follow Steve to Saudi Arabia, where his new job had led him, and wanted to visit her mother before leaving the country. She was excited to visit Iva Mae, and even with the broken ankle, they were planning trips and things to do. Iva Mae was getting a little better with the crutches and would soon be able to move around a little more. One of the first events was a dinner where Denny was receiving the Silver Helmet award from the American Veterans, which is a prestigious award and known as the veterans' Oscar. President Reagan was to be at the event also to receive the Gold Helmet award but was shot days before the event.

> I was in a mess after I broke my ankle. I couldn't get upstairs to get food. The telephone was in the family room, so by the time I would get to the phone they would hang up. Judy was working at the prison and wasn't home. Mike was ten and Brian was five. They came to my help till my daughter Robin came from Kansas City, Missouri.

> Before Mike went to school, he would bring me a breakfast bar and a cup of coffee. Then Brian at noon before he went to kindergarten would bring me two slices of bread, cheese, and an apple. Then at night Mike would bring me cereal. It was a good losing diet. They weren't faring much better than I did.

> Robin came after I had my cast on for two weeks. Steve had left for Saudi Arabia and Robin couldn't go till June. Was I ever glad to see her. I couldn't wash my hair or do anything. She sat in my room and we really had some

good talks. The boys were glad to see her also as she cooked for us all.

I got my long cast off about three weeks after Robin came, and I was dying to go somewhere. So Robin and I went to a movie, but it was a long movie and my leg got so tired.

Now I could go up the stairs with my short cast. I didn't feel so shut in. Robin stayed till the week before I got my cast off, and we really had a good time. We went out to eat, church, and one weekend to Harpers Ferry. While Robin was exploring Harpers Ferry, I sat in the car down by the Potomac River people-watching and looked at magazines. We stayed at the old hotel by the Potomac where Virginia, Maryland, and West Virginia all meet and different presidents have stayed at the hotel.

The hotel is still rustic with no elevator or television, so Robin and I played backgammon that night. This was also where John Brown was hanged during the Civil War.

While Robin was visiting, we attended a banquet in Washington, DC, where my son, Dennis, got the Silver Helmet award. They also gave Alan Cranston a Silver Helmet and President Reagan was supposed to get the Gold Helmet, but this was just after he was shot, so he couldn't attend. I had a long dress on so no one could see my cast and I was walking with a cane. But to my embarrassment they asked me to stand up to introduce me as "Dennis's mom," and it took me forever to get up out of my chair.

I hated to see Robin go home, but I could get up and

down the stairs. Still couldn't drive, but it would be just one week till my cast came off. When I went to get my cast off, I took my shoe to wear home, but behold, my foot was so swollen, I had to wear my cast shoe home. It was summer before I could wear anything but a sandal.

Mike and Brian wanted to know when I was going to break my foot again as I had given them some money for helping me, but I hope to never again have a broken ankle.

ROBIN ANNE GRIFFITHS

Chapter 34

During Iva Mae's years in Washington she learned to explore and learned new ideas and ways of thinking, but after her broken ankle she was a little more careful and stopped going out for walks and doing as much by herself. Denny had remarried and had additional family. His new wife was Jewish, and Iva Mae was introduced to a whole different way of thinking. Julie, Denny's second wife, had three children from a previous marriage, and Iva Mae would spend time with them when she visited their home. They were the age to celebrate their bar and bat mitzvahs, and Iva Mae attended them with the family. She found the ceremony interesting, although she did not understand it and found it confusing. Living in Washington had opened her mind more when it came to religion, and she did not find that she needed to convert Denny's new family, although she knew they would not be going to heaven since they did not believe that Jesus was the savior.

During this time Denny had asked Iva Mae to help him plan a party for fifty guests at his home as a surprise for his wife. Iva Mae planned, shopped, and cooked until the day of the event. It was a big success, and she felt that she had finally had a taste of her dream of owning and running her own restaurant. For years afterward she would tell how she put the dinner together. She would talk about all the food she had prepared and how she had done it with little help and how proud she was of all the compliments she received. Iva Mae had craved attention and praise from others all her life. Her motto in many of her relationships for most of her years was "They like me," whether the person was a new friend, acquaintance, government official, or professional executive who came into her life. Her requirement for attention and approval as she aged became more important to her emotional feeling of being needed and loved.

While living in the capital, Iva Mae had many opportunities to meet government officials and celebrities. She wrote Robin a letter telling about her visit to the White House for a dinner. The first couple of pages of the letter talked about the evening meal, meeting different government officials at the event, and the different rooms within the house. But the most exciting part of the evening was being introduced to Kirk Douglas. She then wrote four pages about all her favorite movies that he was in and how he really did have that distinctive dimple in his chin, how nice he was to her, and that she would never forget shaking his hand and the look in his eyes. Yes, Iva Mae was star-struck. Kirk Douglas was the leading man in movies from her young adulthood, and she got to actually meet him.

In 1982 she received the surprising news from Tammy that she was going to be a grandmother again. It was a difficult call, because at twenty-two, Tammy still did not have a good relationship with her mother and was still floundering in many aspects of her life. She was living in Maplewood, Missouri, with Sandy. Maplewood is a charming neighborhood town within St. Louis County. Sandy had purchased an old two-story home that had a Victorian feel to it and was built in the late 1800s. It had a full attic and basement and needed many repairs, since the wiring, plumbing, and other items were from the original construction or from many years earlier. The home sat up on a hill and had three bedrooms and an old-style bathroom with a claw-foot tub. It had large rooms and a lot of space from the high ceilings, and wood floors.

Tammy was single, and her lifestyle had been pretty wild. She did not realize at first that she was pregnant and was in complete denial about the matter. Tammy had been overweight since childhood, so her pregnancy did not show. Sandy figured it out and finally forced her to face the situation and see a physician. When Tammy first found out she was pregnant, it was in question if she would keep the baby. Sandy even thought of adopting the baby and raising the child as her own. But Tammy decided that she wanted this child and would be the mother.

Sandy agreed to help Tammy but insisted she call their mother with the news. Iva Mae took the news well overall. She was concerned for Tammy and didn't believe she would be able to handle the responsibilities, but she was excited at the prospect of a new grandbaby. The fact that Tammy was an unwed mother was not the embarrassment or the shame that had been attached to Sandy years earlier. Being in the environment of Washington, DC, had showed Iva Mae that many people had different lifestyles and were happy, productive, and living full lives without the stigma of hell and damnation or the religious consequences she had been accustomed to in the Bible Belt of the Midwest in her earlier life.

Although Iva Mae was more open to this new way of looking at the fact that her daughter was going to be an unwed mother, she still found it difficult to talk to her friends in Missouri about it and worried what they thought of her having a daughter in this situation. Amber June, a beautiful little girl named after Tammy's best friend from childhood, Barbara June, was born at the beginning of the following year, and Iva Mae made a trip back to Missouri to see her new grandchild. Although their relationship was still volatile at best, Tammy and her mother kept boundaries for the most part during the visit while Iva Mae enjoyed a new baby girl in the family.

It was not long after Amber was born that Sandy became pregnant. Amber had brought back more than ever the need and desire for a child in her life that was hers and hers alone. She planned the pregnancy and the responsibility of raising the child alone as a single parent. The following December, James Reginald (Reggie) was born, and Iva Mae was at the hospital upon his arrival.

Iva Mae was taking these new changes in stride and accepting that these were her grandchildren and they needed her love and attention. She had been feeling unhappy in Washington with the changes that had taken place in her son's family. She had been toying with the thought of moving to Florida to live with her brother Raymond and his wife, Mildred, when it was suggested she move to St. Louis and help Sandy and Tammy with their children. Although she worried for Mike and Brian, she felt that her job with them was over and that her help and influence would no longer make a difference or change. So she packed up her belongings and moved back to Missouri to a new city and life with her daughters and grandchildren.

This was difficult at best, as Iva Mae was now in a new city, without any of her anchors of friends or church. At sixty years of age, she found that changes were becoming harder for her to undertake. She did not care for St. Louis as a city. She first moved into an apartment, but after her lifestyle in Washington she felt that she had stepped backward and was losing ground in her standard of living. The building was in an old neighborhood near Sandy's home. It had four apartments in it, each with a living room, bedroom, kitchen, and bathroom. Each apartment had a storage area in the basement. The rooms were large, but the buildings were old.

Iva Mae didn't really feel safe, and money along with security was a worry once again. Denny was good to her and provided generous monthly checks to help her. Sandy also helped with finances since she was taking care of two babies. Sandy's job with the railroad kept her working on different shifts, and her schedule was often changed. Tammy's work kept her busy and perhaps a bit more scheduled. Sandy and Iva Mae were on the go a lot even with the small children, as both of them liked to shop and go out to eat and do things in the city. All that being said, Iva Mae was tied down more than ever with the small children, and although she loved Reggie and Amber and thought her role in their life was most important, her days of freedom had been removed by a toddler and a baby.

Chapter 35

In September 1984, Robin and Steve planned a month-long train trip across Europe, starting in Amsterdam and ending in Athens, and asked Iva Mae if she would like to go as their guest. Denny offered to pay for her airfare, and after much planning over several months, she was off to meet them, flying from St. Louis to Amsterdam. This was the biggest trip Iva Mae, at sixty-two, had ever dreamed of taking. She was going overseas by herself and was anxious about everything going well when she landed. This kept her worried throughout the entire flight to the point that she got very little sleep. As always, Iva Mae had a need to talk to people and easily met a girl on the flight to whom she could talk about anything and everything that came to her mind. It was helpful to her to be able to express her worries and brag about her children to others. It calmed her if she felt that she had made a friend and they liked her.

Although the world was in its usual turmoil, Europe was fairly calm. The plan was to begin in Amsterdam and end in Athens, with all travel being done by train with a Eurail pass and then ferry passage between Italy and Greece.

Iva Mae's flight was an hour late, and she worried that she would somehow miss her daughter and son-in-law, but they met her at the airport in Holland. The weather was beautiful and the temperature perfect. They got a taxi from the airport and went straight into downtown Amsterdam to a wonderful hotel in the central part of the old town right across from the Royal Palace. After registering and getting their luggage settled into the room, they were off on their adventure, starting with a walk in the area, seeing a puppet show and a parade in the Dam Square of central Amsterdam, and then visiting the Royal Palace, which had been the home of King Louis Napoleon and later of the Dutch Royal House. Seeing a beautiful structure full of history and incredible art was a good start to Iva Mae's first day on foreign soil.

That evening they went on a candlelight cruise on the canals. The boat was glass enclosed, and the service was impeccable, with a variety of cheeses and wine. Iva Mae enjoyed the cheese and even tasted the Oppenheimer Scholl Rhine wine. Her favorite part of the evening was on the way back to the hotel. The bus driver had enjoyed himself too much and was a little drunk, and Iva Mae thought that was the funniest and best part of the day as she watched the reactions of the people on the bus from the evening's fun. She kept a diary throughout her travels so she'd be able to look back on her memories and enjoy the trip again.

Amsterdam weather was cool and nice. We went on a boat canal tour during the day and had a light lunch on the boat, then a tour through a diamond factory. It was interesting because the boat actually went out of the canals and into the North Sea for a bit. In the afternoon we went through Anne Frank's house, which was interesting and is now a museum. It had a very strange feeling to the place going behind the bookcase doorway into the place they had hidden for so long. A sad story and I remember much of the book as I looked at their life. Afterward that evening we ate at a Japanese restaurant at the hotel. The food was so good and I learned to eat with chopsticks, and that was fun because the waiter liked and helped me. The waiter had a rubber band around them to help to hold the sticks. We all laughed and laughed at me dropping the food back on the plate. It sure was hard to eat fast! The evening ended with a walk through the Red Light District, and I will have to be sure to tell my friends about that experience, plus I kept my eye on Steve to make sure he didn't disappear. We had to pack that evening so we could get an early start to the train station the next morning for our next stop in Paris.

It was raining when we left Amsterdam, and it was still

raining when we got to Paris. The train ride was nice and comfortable. Once we got to Paris, we had trouble getting a hotel when we were at the station, and you can't believe the crowds. We had to stand in line for a long time waiting to see where we may stay while in the city, as we didn't have any reservations. On the way to the hotel in the taxi, we saw Notre Dame, the Seine River, and we passed the Louvre museum.

After settling into the hotel, which was not as nice as the one in Holland, we went for a walk and found a street vendor making strawberry crepes, which were so good. We have a busy schedule for tomorrow with all the places we want to see, and my feet are swollen from either too much salt or walking. The hotel in Paris was more of an old home turned into a hotel. It had very high ceilings, but the rooms were put together in an odd way that made me think of a rooming house. I didn't sleep good because the bed was uncomfortable.

The next morning we went to the top of the Eiffel Tower, which was fun because you could see all over the city. When we left there, we headed to the Louvre, where I saw the Mona Lisa and the Venus de Milo and many other famous pieces, which were interesting. We had a good dinner at a French restaurant, then shopped. I bought a handkerchief and three scarves. That evening we went to the Moulin Rouge, which is a dinner theater. It was good, but funny because we were right in front of the stage, and the performing women were topless. I tasted French red and white wine and had champagne. We went to bed very late and had to get up early the next morning.

We left Paris the next morning at seven. It was cloudy and drizzling. We traveled by train and had to change at Zurich, Switzerland. It had snowed, and we could see the ski slopes from our train platform. The train ride is wonderful. Before we got to our next change at Chur, it started snowing and the Alps are beautiful. We also saw the Rhine River. We took a smaller train at Chur. It traveled all the way up to the top to a small town called Arosa, a small resort town. Once there we had a reservation at the nicest hotel where you could see the Alps and the snow was about twelve inches. That evening we had an interesting dinner because I didn't know what I was eating but it was good. You just can't believe how beautiful it is up here. I just love it.

The following day we took a horse and carriage and saw the countryside. Robin and I washed some clothes by hand, and we just sat around and relaxed. We decided to stay an extra day here because it is so beautiful and nice. Breakfast and dinner is included with our hotel stay. The breakfast consisted of crescent rolls, different breads, ham, cheese, jelly, juice, coffee, and other pastries. They had a dish which looks like oatmeal but isn't. Our dinner took us two hours, as they are served in courses. It was by candlelight and very good. I tasted their red and white wine. I loved their beds here; the blankets are like mattresses and so warm. Plus the hot chocolate here is delicious.

Since we decided to stay longer, we had to change hotels, but I ended up with even a nicer room with a better view. We went to town to shop and I bought a plate for my collection and found Sandy a music box for her collection. Once we got back to the hotel, we went swimming in the indoor pool, then into the spa's hot tub, which wasn't very hot. The dinner that evening was good, and while we were at dinner, the staff came to my room to lay the covers back on the bed and leave some candy. They even had my nightgown on the bed. I am really getting the royal treatment here. It is certainly a beautiful place, but the hills are hard to climb. I love the Alps.

The following day at breakfast I had my choice of crescent rolls, a variety of breads, juices, jellies, cheese, and ham plus a lot more. Afterward I walked to town and met Steve and Robin. There was a bicycle race coming in for the finish and we walked around to window-shop. That afternoon we went for a horse and buggy ride, which was fun and we saw some beautiful scenery. That evening we had a five-course dinner, and the salad was unusual because it was sherbet with brandy and I think more brandy than sherbet. The dessert was good, too— raspberries with ice cream. We leave tomorrow on the train heading to Salzburg, Austria.

We arrived in Salzburg and it is as pretty as Switzerland. We have a nice hotel, which is definitely Austrian. It's a very old home that was made into a bed-and-breakfast owned and run by Anna and Otto. When we arrived, they served us coffee and homemade apple strudel. It was chilly out, and we sat outside on the patio. The strudel was delicious, and it warmed us up as we looked out over the city and the fall day.

After we settled in, we decided to go explore the city a little. The city has a fort or castle high on top of the town, which was built in 1077, and we decided to walk up to look around. I got three quarters of the way but couldn't go any further. I hyperventilated and had to sit and wait on Robin and Steve. Once we walked down, we stopped and had a delicious typical Austrian dinner of salad, and dumplings with ham and cheese. On our way back to the hotel we walked by the place known to be where "Silent Night" was written.

The next day was very exciting because we went on the *Sound of Music* tour, which was three and a half hours and one of my favorite movies. They showed us all the places it was filmed plus other things interesting like a church that held ten thousand people, Dragon Mountain, an underpass built by hand, beautiful countryside, and the church where Julie Andrews's character's marriage ceremony was filmed and Mozart's home and museum.

Afterward we came back to the city and had lunch and shopped. We did go up to the fort or castle, which was never taken by other forces, but this time we took the tram. We went to a casino that was on the side of the mountain down from the fort and had dinner looking out over the city. I am tired, as we walked and walked. They use coarse pink toilet paper everywhere here, and you have to pay to go to the bathroom.

We started out on the train again the following day, but this time we were not hurried and on the way to Florence, Italy, and warmer weather. We came through the Alps, then through tunnels from the Adriatic side to the Mediterranean side. I think how it would have been some trip with the elephants that Hannibal had crossing the

Alps. It was a long trip and we got a hotel across from the train station once we arrived. That evening we had spaghetti and wine for dinner, and afterward we were all tired, so went back to the hotel and bed. It was very noisy here from all the traffic, and we were up high in the hotel, so I could see everyone on the street. I am nervous here, as you have to watch everyone on account of the pickpockets.

The following day we went to the Florence Baptistery and the Altar of St. John, then to the cathedral, which is the main church in Florence. Afterward we went to the river and the Ponte Vecchio, where the silver and gold market shops are on the bridge that was originally built during Roman times. Afterward we went to the Accademia Gallery to see the marble statue of David that Michelangelo had finished over four hundred years ago, which was outstanding.

We shopped and ate. The food was good and the waiter serenaded me after dinner. I don't know what he sang, but it was fun. We tasted all the wines and beer. The streets are so crowded and busy.

The next day we went to Pisa to see the Leaning Tower. The train ride was different, crowded, and not as clean. The Leaning Tower is really leaning. Robin and Steve walked up to the top, and I started to but changed my mind after the first flight. The space was small and the steps were so worn, they dipped. I went to the cathedral to wait. Afterward we had lunch and shopped a little. It was fun watching people take their picture with the tower. We rode a bus from the train station, and as we boarded the bus to return, we saw an argument between an American and an Italian. The American called the other a bastard three times, and the Italian would spit on the American each time. Once we were all on the bus, the Italian stood in front and spit on the bus, then yelled at us all. It was quite a show.

Ordering breakfast the next morning before we left for Rome was funny. We ordered juice, bread, and coffee and got boiled eggs, bread, and coffee. The train to Rome was fast and clean and a good trip. We got a taxi to the hotel, which was very beautiful and expensive on a hill above the city. Rome is a big place, a very big place with lots of people. Everywhere in Italy has been busy and crowded. Food is expensive here too. They charge so much at the hotel that we went out and bought food at a local market. But the things to see are incredible. We went to see the Coliseum, which was built in 72 AD, and we walked through the Roman Forum, Tomb of the Unknown Soldier, the Spanish Steps, and the Fountain of Trevi, which I made sure to throw change in and drank from so I will return. We walked a lot, so much that I offered to pay for a taxi. It's crowded and people drive crazy. It's a very old and interesting place.

One of my favorite sights was going to St. Peter's. It was beautiful and I kept thinking about Peter being buried under the church. Michelangelo's work is everywhere here, from the guards' uniforms to the dome in the church and then the Sistine Chapel and the *Last Judgment*. It was beautiful. The statue of St. Peter where people have knelt to kiss his feet is worn away.

After our time in Rome, we left to go to the coast to Brindisi, which is a port town. It was a very long ride, about nine hours. I met a couple from New York who rode with us, and I enjoyed their company. On the train ride we saw the Mediterranean Sea, and once we got to the town, we took a taxi to the dock to board a ferry. It was a long way to get from the taxi to the check-in and then to the boat. We had to carry our luggage, and it was almost too much for me. We left at night and we slept some, but the seats were like being in a plane and not too comfortable. It was a long day and we are all tired. We are crossing the Adriatic Sea to Greece. The ferry is full of commercial and tourist people and vehicles, and it's crowded and we will be on the boat for about twenty hours.

At five the next day we went out to see the ship dock at Corfu. I was feeling a little seasick, so I slept a lot during the trip, and we finally arrived and got off the boat in Patros, Greece. It was a little town, and we got a room on the Adriatic Sea, and the people there were so nice. We walked and had dinner; it was my first time eating moussaka with a Greek salad, which was good. Back at the hotel afterward, we could hear the boats docking.

The next day we caught the train heading to Athens. It was quite the ride for four and a half hours—packed in like sardines, including some small farm animals, and very smelly. Once in Athens, we looked for a taxi to get to Glyfada, a town by the sea where we were staying. One man offered to take us but wanted Robin and I to ride in the back of his pickup. It is beautiful here, and we had a very good dinner of Greek salad, pizza and tzatziki by the

Aegean Sea. I am very tired now. I will be here for five days, and so far I like Greece, and I like it much better than Italy.

We went shopping the next day, and there are a lot of shops and what they call a huge flea market. Robin and Steve were expecting their friends Ellen and Tim from Saudi Arabia to fly in that day, and we were checking if they had arrived. I love the food here, but it's funny because I ordered lemonade and got Sprite, and when I ordered an orange drink, I got lemonade.

It's very warm here, but we have a room on the fourth floor with a breeze and good view of the area, including the sea and many ships and boats. When we went into Athens the following day, we saw the Acropolis and the Parthenon, Hadrian's Arch of Triumph, and the Temple of Zeus. We walked a lot, including the Plaka and the unknown tomb. I tried grape leaves at lunch, which were not good.

I don't care much for Ellen and Tim, and their son Adam, their three-year-old, is spoiled. It takes a half day to go anywhere because they have to stop often for drinks. We did go to the beach that afternoon and even played on the paddleboats, and it was fun but a topless beach. I don't think anyone looks cute without clothes—weird! That night I kept Adam at the hotel while everyone went out on the town. They didn't get home till three thirty that morning. We had reservations to go out on a boat the next day to several islands. It was windy and the Aegean Sea was wild. Everyone was hung over from the night before and feeling sick with the boat rocking. We went to

Hydra, and I could see the cannons that protected the harbor. It's a small island with no cars. Poros was next, and it was more modern. Aegina was next and was the greenest of the islands and a big fishing industry. The day was not much fun, as everyone was so hung over.

I leave tomorrow and it's been a good trip. It was a wonderful gift from Denny, Robin, and Steve. Tammy and Sandy helped with getting me ready too. I got ready early the next day and we left for the airport. Robin and Steve said their goodbyes at the gate. I will really miss them. I took a bus to the airplane, and during the flight home we went across England and the Shannon River in Ireland. Got through customs in New York and took a plane to Washington, DC, where I was able to see everyone before going back to Missouri. What a trip and lifetime memories.

Chapter 36

The trip across Europe with Iva Mae was bittersweet for Robin. For the first time Robin was seeing her mother aging. She enjoyed being able to give her mother this gift but was torn by the conflict she felt at the same time. Iva Mae could not just enjoy the trip without reminding everyone that this was her funeral trip. She talked continually about the money being spent and how that would have paid for her funeral. She brought it up multiple times and felt she had to share it with anyone she sat next to on the train. Robin finally told her that she didn't want to hear about her funeral anymore, which made Iva Mae cry and Robin feel sorry and guilty. In Austria, when Iva Mae had difficulty on the walk to the fortress, Robin was greatly concerned about her mother's health, compounded by Iva Mae's continual comments about her funeral.

Iva Mae's need for attention was beginning to be more apparent during this trip as well. She needed to have people like her, and anyone who showed her the least bit of attention was a new friend who "liked her." She spent much of the time complaining about how living in St. Louis with Sandy and Tammy was tiring and they were taking advantage of her with the children. She felt that she had lost the life she had enjoyed in Washington. She could see only the now and not the whole picture of how she had not been happy when she left Washington. She had a very narrow view of how her needs were not being met, however skewed they were.

Robin did see that her mother was in need of a life again outside of caring for the grandchildren. Once she moved to St. Louis, her life had changed. She did not have friends with whom she could go to lunch or shopping. She did not make friends with her neighbors, and commented frequently how they were not her type. She did not have a church, and with Sandy and Tammy's schedule it was hard to plan time for outings or church. As a result, Iva Mae began to listen more to preachers on television and rely on Sandy for her friendship, fun, and entertainment.

Iva Mae took great pride in Amber and Reggie. She would tell everyone how she was raising them and making sure they were given the right upbringing. She especially loved telling anyone who would listen how Reggie was such a serious baby and she was the first to see him smile. She knew at that moment that she was special to him. She was determined that both of these children would have the right teachings about God and that she would be special in their lives.

After Iva Mae returned from her trip to Europe, Bob passed away. Robin received a call one morning in Saudi Arabia from Bob's wife, Lois, that her father was not doing well and was in the hospital. Robin had kept in touch with her father over the years since her parents had divorced. She would visit Bob each time she was traveling to visit family. Her relationship with her father was the closest of all the children, and she was grateful that she had him as part of her family. That evening she received a second call that he had died. Bob had been suffering with medical issues over the last several years. He had had circulation problem for many years, then developed diabetes. Over the years his habits were catching up to him. Although Bob was still tall, more lean than not, and active, his smoking and working environments, along with poor eating habits, had taken a toll.

Lois had been good for Bob. She cared for him, and they had both enjoyed the same type of lifestyle. They would go fishing together and had a small patch of land where Bob planted a garden, and Lois would cook the rewards of his efforts. Bob had started breeding and training beagles for hunting in the last five years of his life and took great joy in showing them off to anyone who stopped by to visit. Lois had changed their diet to accommodate Bob's medical needs, and he seemed to be doing better for the last year of his life. The cause of his death was ruled to be his heart just giving out. He was seventy-four years of age when he passed away.

Robin and Steve immediately made arrangements to fly back to the States. After a long trip they finally landed in St. Louis for a layover before their final flight to Springfield. Sandy, Tammy, and Iva Mae, along with the children, met them at the airport and took them to dinner while they waited for their next flight. Sandy was not going to the funeral, as her relationship with Bob had been gone for many years. Tammy planned to attend, even though she and her father had not spoken for several years. She, Iva Mae, and Amber would be driving down before the funeral. Iva Mae didn't plan to attend the service but would care for Amber while Tammy attended with Robin.

During their dinner, Iva Mae had a great need to tell everyone how Bob had not been a good husband and how hard he had been to live with because of his drinking and not working enough, plus many other negative comments. It appeared she was justifying her life and why she had divorced him. Robin was really devastated from her father's death. This was her first real experience dealing with the loss of a loved one, and she had had a good relationship with her father. It hurt her to hear her mother's remarks.

Iva Mae wanted to go to Springfield to hear about the service, and she knew that Denny would be flying in as well and that she would be able to see him. Iva Mae was really quite nosey and always wanted to be the center of attention, so this would provide an opportunity to hear about the service and be with her children. While in town she would be able to see friends and tell them about Bob's death, and share her stories concerning her difficult life with him.

It was a fast three days once Robin arrived in Springfield. Lois had waited so that Robin could make the arrangements. A traditional visitation was held the evening before the funeral. Denny remarked how Bob would have liked it because next to the casket, two of his old buddies were telling fishing and hunting tales. Bob's family from Arkansas came up for the service. His son, Burnice, did not attend, saying he did not have enough time off from work to make the trip. Those of Bob's first family who attended included a couple of sisters, a daughter, and a grandchild, who kept to themselves and were gone as soon as the service was over.

It was a typical open-casket service with a clergyman officiating. Once it was over, the family rode in a funeral procession to the cemetery atop a hill outside of town. It was there that Bob was laid to rest on an overcast fall day with leaves beginning to drop from the trees.

Iva Mae wanted to know all the details, which Tammy supplied to satisfy her curiosity. Bob did not have many possessions, and Robin received a few—his Bible and his railroad pocket watch as well as an antique tin box with painting brushes—for her memories of a father she loved and would dearly miss.

Iva Mae really enjoyed her short stay in Springfield. She missed the city and considered it her home, as she had lived there so long. She visited with friends and enjoyed their company, talking about the past, church, and her life with her grandchildren.

ROBIN ANNE GRIFFITHS

Chapter 37

The 1980s had brought new changes to Iva Mae's world.
She had begun to talk more about the Second Coming
of her Lord. She would tell her children the signs were
there, just like the Bible said, especially in the book of
Revelation. The news reflected the predictions every day. By
1985 there was famine in Ethiopia, and terrorism was on the
rise, with attacks in Europe and the Middle East. The spread of
AIDS had many in the population scared, and the government

began to screen blood donations. The eighties music industry had shifted to hair bands with their long teased locks and the debut of MTV, with Michael Jackson's *Thriller* skyrocketing to the top of the charts. *Yuppies* became a household word describing upwardly mobile young professionals. There was a focus on wealth and consumption that included displaying it openly and conspicuously.

Sandy had an opportunity to transfer her job and move back to Springfield. She decided to make the change, knowing it would be a better environment for her, her son, and her mother. Tammy and Amber were also part of the move, as Tammy was not tied to any situation or job. Sandy found a rental house, and she and Iva Mae moved into it along with Reggie. Tammy wanted to go to school to get her degree, and she asked Robin and Steve if she and Amber, age three at the time, could move in with them while she studied at Clemson University in South Carolina.

Before moving, Tammy and Iva Mae went to see the new Steven Spielberg film *The Color Purple*. Tammy had read the book, and Iva Mae had not. It was showing at the nearest theater in St. Louis, and off the two of them went, as was their habit on a weekend afternoon. The theater was packed, and after buying their popcorn and sodas, they found their seats. Iva Mae commented a little too loudly to Tammy about how many black people were at the movies, and Tammy then knew this had been a bad idea. Iva Mae had few filters when in public. If she needed to purchase something, she rarely saw her surroundings and would move to the front of the line. She just did not see that others were waiting. If she noticed something that struck her, she spoke her thoughts out loud before thinking about who might hear her. Iva Mae spent the time during the movie commenting about how certain situations were similar to her growing up and directed several questions to Tammy. Tammy wanted to crawl under the chair and find a way out of the building but instead told her mother to be quiet and that she would explain later.

Later during this year Iva Mae and Tammy were watching *Oprah* when Oprah Winfrey opened up about her abusive childhood. Iva Mae told Tammy that she had had a similar experience with her father. She didn't go into details, and Tammy, shocked, didn't ask too many questions. Iva Mae didn't elaborate but made it clear that after her mother had died, her father had behaved inappropriately with her.

Several months after Iva Mae, Sandy, and Reggie moved to Springfield, Sandy found a home on the south side of town to purchase, and they moved again. This house was a ranch-style two-bedroom with a two-car garage on a quiet street at the end of a cul-de-sac. It had a big fenced-in backyard and shade trees, including a weeping willow in the front yard. The house felt very familiar to Iva Mae, because it was similar to one she had lived in with Bob, and she liked the neighborhood.

Iva Mae was happy to be back in what had become her town. She had begun many years earlier comparing Springfield with anywhere she was visiting, and Springfield always seemed to be the better of the two. She connected with her old friends and began to make new ones almost immediately. Church was a center point of her life again, and she found a large congregation that made her feel welcomed and special.

Within a year, Iva Mae and Sandy agreed that she needed to have her own place. She was creating her own life with friends and needed space. Sandy also found that she wanted to have time and space as well, in order to keep her sanity. They began to look and found a lower-income apartment complex just a few blocks away, right next to the shopping mall. It was a six-story austere brown-and-tan building with a covered circle drive in front and parking in the back. The building residents were mainly elderly, and Iva Mae would talk about the "old" people, as she was only sixty-four at the time and did not consider herself old. With the help of Sandy and friends Wayne and Helen, she moved into the fourth-floor apartment, a one-bedroom and bath with the living and dining areas together. The kitchen was small but perfect for her needs. The rooms were large, with big picture windows and good storage areas. Sandy helped Iva Mae decorate by hanging her plate collection and buying furniture at garage sales and Goodwill as well as special accent items to make it homey.

Iva Mae's friend Helen remembers the move with this story:

> We had Reggie with us and had a key to the elevator to use for getting things upstairs to the apartment. I thought Reggie was with Iva Mae, and she thought he was with me. Anyway, he got on the elevator by himself and got the key turned on and then stalled between floors. There was a couple in charge of the building, but the man was gone and the woman had no idea what to do, but since Wayne had worked on elevators, the situation was taken care of quickly. Understandably Reggie was pretty upset, being only three years old.

After that, Iva Mae was always watchful of the children, afraid she would be in trouble at the complex and lose her apartment.

Iva Mae loved her new apartment. She had a sofa that made into a bed so she could have overnight guests, and often she would have a relative visit. Reggie spent most Saturday evenings and overnight with her. A few years later, Tammy and Amber returned to Springfield, and Amber would then have weekend sleepovers with her grandmother too. These visits were special for all of them, as Iva Mae would make sure to have their favorite food, books, television, and other entertainment. They shared stories and feelings and had a very close bond.

During this time, Iva Mae really began to cook again, especially during the holidays, when she made cookies, candy, peanut brittle, and fudge to send to all her children, grandchildren, and other relatives as Christmas gifts. It was a quest to find all the ingredients needed at the least expensive cost. The next hunt was to find containers to put the gifts in: they had to be a reasonable price yet able to hold the freshness for at least a while. Years earlier, Sandy had believed Iva Mae needed hobbies to keep her busy, so she had introduced different things over the years. They had taken many classes together, including crocheting. Iva Mae had crocheted afghans for each family member over the years, including baby ones for any time she needed a baby shower gift. At Sandy's urging, she also wrote stories about her life growing up. Now Sandy had her in a class to learn how to quilt, and she was planning all the quilts she would make for each of her children and grandchildren. She was busy with all her hobbies, socializing, and church. For the most part she was happy, but throughout her life, she was always looking for something that was missing. That missing piece was the part that had her look for others to like her and give her happiness.

Traveling was still part of Iva Mae's life. She and her friends would go on day, overnight, and weekend trips. She also occasionally took a trip with Denny as he traveled to different speaking engagements. Iva Mae still loved to get out and about, and she and Sandy took every opportunity to explore and see the most they could around them.

Sandy's favorite story was about how her mother loved to be on the go:

> One of my favorite stories Mom has always told on herself happened when she was a youngster of maybe six or seven years of age. She always wanted to go with her brothers and their friends everywhere they went. One day the boys were planning a trip and would not let Iva Mae go with them. In usual little sister fashion she cried, pleaded, threw a fit, and did not give up. Finally the boys relented and told her she could go with them, but they were leaving immediately.
>
> Now, we all know that if you are going out, you must wear clean underwear. I mean, what if you were in a wreck and had to go to the hospital? So Iva Mae raced to her room to change clothes and threw her dirty clothes every which way. Unfortunately her dirty underwear landed on the curtain rods. She didn't have time to worry with them, because the boys were about to leave; besides she couldn't reach them. But how dismayed she was when big sister Mary would not get her underwear off the curtain rod and left them there as extra decoration for several days.
>
> You can always count on Iva Mae to be ready to GO. I remember a time when I was about six or seven years old, and my cousin told Iva Mae about a fortune-teller. They decided it was very important to see what the future held

for them. She did the swipe with a washcloth, changed clothes, and they were off in a cloud of dust.

She may be better about throwing her clothes around, but she is always ready to go. We have been to Yellowstone National Park, Carlsbad Caverns, and Mesa Verde National Park; ridden the Silverton Steam Train in Colorado; done Nashville, St. Louis, Baltimore, and DC; traipsed through Disney World, SeaWorld, and Six Flags; tent camped, stayed in cheap motels, roughed it, and even booked a few nice motels. We have had breakfast in the park, picnics at the creek, and even lunch in the US Capitol dining room.

Iva Mae 65th Birthday

Chapter 38

The Christmas of 1986, Iva Mae planned to visit Robin and Steve in South Carolina while Tammy and Amber were still living with them. It was exciting, as the entire visit reminded Iva Mae of the Christmas holidays when her children were young. The fifty-year-old brick home was small and in the oldest part of the historical area, surrounded by hills and trees. It had two fireplaces, and although it was small, the rooms were large.

There were presents everywhere in the living room on Christmas morning—so many that it was hard to walk through the room. The morning started with waking the children up with Iva Mae's homemade cinnamon rolls and hot chocolate. After the gifts were opened, the big dinner was in preparation until late afternoon while Amber and Reggie were busy playing with all their new toys. At the end of the day, when all the wrapping paper was picked up and the dishes were clean, Iva Mae commented on how the day reminded her how much she enjoyed Christmas.

Sandy, Reggie, and I were living in Springfield while Steve, Robin, Tammy, and Amber were living in Greenville, South Carolina, so Reggie and I decided to go spend Christmas with them. Sandy had to work and Reggie had just turned four years old. I had a nearly new car that Denny had got for me for my upcoming sixty-fifth birthday. The thing that worried me most about the trip was the weather. I also didn't know if Reggie would be good during the drive. It is about eight or nine hundred miles, and you stay in a motel one night.

We started out, and Reggie was in the backseat and me in the front. I fixed snacks and a drink with a straw, and I kept this in the front with me so it was handy. We started out at six in the morning. We got along pretty good and he didn't get cranky till I got almost to Nashville. Then he finally took a nap. We made it on the other side of Nashville to a motel about six o'clock that evening. We went to eat and they fixed Reggie what he wanted: one pancake, one egg, and one sausage. He never forgot about the place.

We got to Robin's the next day. Amber and Reggie were glad to see each other, and they were excited about Christmas morning. Christmas Eve we all went to Asheville, North Carolina, to the Biltmore Estate to see the Christmas decorations and listen to the singers performing Christmas carols. It was so pretty. I saw the biggest Christmas tree I had ever seen. We enjoyed it and then went out to eat. Once home we put the little ones to bed so they could get up early for Santa Claus.

Next day there were so many presents, it took us till noon to open them all. The kids were so excited. We had all the coffee we could drink, and the kids had hot chocolate. Robin fixed a turkey and we had a big feast that evening.

I had planned on staying to celebrate Amber's fifth birthday at the Show Biz Pizza place. We were going to have that early so we could go home. I had also brought her a bicycle for her birthday, which was her first bike.

The day we were going home, it came the biggest snow that Greenville had had in fifty years. No one could go anywhere. Reggie and Amber had fun playing in the snow. Steve built a fire in the fireplace, and Reggie and I slept in the front of the fire, which he thought was fun.

We had to stay another week, and then Steve had trouble getting my car to the main road. We waited till afternoon to start the trip home so the ice would be melting. On our way we saw cars in the ditch, but Reggie was so good, and we got along way down the road. We stopped just seventy-five miles before Nashville. It was supposed to be bad the next day. I prayed it wouldn't be too bad. I got up and we had some ice, but only the bridges were supposed to be bad. Reggie and I had breakfast at McDonald's and started out about eight that morning. He was good again and we didn't stop but only for the bathroom and to eat at noon and get gas.

It was dark when we got home, but Sandy had a big kettle of soup, which was delicious. Reggie was glad to see his mom. I was really glad to be home. We had a wonderful time at Robin's. Enjoyed Tammy and Amber, but I was nervous about the weather. It makes me think twice about driving on any trips in the winter. They had also had a big ice storm in Springfield with no electricity that same time.

The following spring, not long after Iva Mae's visit to Greenville, Tammy and Amber moved back to Springfield and in with Sandy once again. Tammy had decided that she was not going to continue with her education. She had been going to school a long time and was not finishing her degree, although she had enough credits for almost two degrees. She was having a hard time dealing with Robin and Steve's rules, and the house was too small for three adults, a five-year-old, and two large dogs. The drive to Clemson and being a single mother was just too much for her, and she felt that Amber needed more than what she could afford in Greenville. She would start over in Springfield, and with Sandy and her mother, she would have more opportunities for work and for Amber. Sandy once again opened her home to Tammy and Amber, and Iva Mae began to watch Amber with Reggie while their mothers worked.

Amber and Reggie both started school that fall. Most often Iva Mae was in charge of getting the children to school and staying with them afterward. She fixed their lunches and took them to any activity they were involved with during the school year.

Sandy and Tammy were both working and were grateful that their mother was available to handle the details of school life other than the parent-teacher meetings and special occasions.

Iva Mae was also determined to have her grandchildren know Jesus and be saved, so she made it a point to take them to church each Sunday and have them involved in the programs and plays as part of their upbringing. She had become a member of South Haven Baptist Church and immediately started a whole new collection of friendships. Amber and Reggie were with her most Sundays and knew as many of the members as their grandmother. Iva Mae met one of her closest friends at this church. Vivian came into Iva Mae's life like she was her sister, and their friendship continued throughout their lives without one cross word or any hurt feelings.

For the most part Iva Mae felt life was good. She worried much of the time about many things, as had become her habit. Her relationship with Sandy was good for the most part. She had learned to not push too far when Sandy became agitated. They had mostly unspoken boundaries with each other and about the rearing of Reggie. Iva Mae enjoyed spending time with them, although she sometimes didn't like their lifestyle or beliefs. Sandy's decision to have a child without a father's involvement bothered her, although Iva Mae did not care for Reggie's father or the way the event had come about. She did not like that Sandy was not involved in church. Both Reggie and Amber were baptized as babies at a Lutheran church while they lived in St. Louis. This was Sandy's idea, and Iva Mae never agreed with the ceremony, although she did not say anything to either of her daughters. Sandy's way of taking care of her home was another issue with Iva Mae. Sandy had piles of things all around the house. She did not like to clean and did not dust often, which also bothered her mother.

On the other hand, Iva Mae's relationship with Tammy was volatile and strained at best. Iva Mae had never understood her daughter and why she just couldn't change her thoughts and ways. Tammy enjoyed getting her mother riled up and putting her on the defensive. She would play devil's advocate much of the time. One of their conversations was about Iva Mae's favorite subject—death and the Second Coming. She told Tammy that neither she nor anyone else should be cremated, as it was against God's will. If you were cremated, you could not go to heaven when the Lord came back to take the souls that had already passed. Tammy of course could not resist this easy argument and asked her mother to explain what would happen to a family that had been in a terrible car accident and completely burned up. Would they not go to heaven? With that comment, Iva Mae's mouth snapped shut and she dropped the subject with a "Humph."

The following July, Iva Mae turned sixty-five, and Sandy planned a surprise birthday party for her at her home. She invited all the relatives, many of whom Iva Mae had not seen in many years, to a cookout in the backyard. She told Iva that she had invited a few friends over for a cookout and to come to the house at a certain time. Denny had planned a visit, so she was excited that he was going to be in town and that he was bringing both of his boys. Her relationship with Brian and Mike had been special to her, having lived with them and helped bring them up for many years. Robin told her that she had a last-minute work event in Kansas City so she would be able to stop in over the weekend to see her from South Carolina. Iva Mae did not suspect a thing but a family cookout.

When she arrived that day, everyone was in the backyard waiting, including her only surviving siblings and older brothers, Raymond and Emmett. Emmett was now nearly ninety years old but still in good health. Her brother Pete had passed away four years earlier. A photograph was taken of them together as had traditionally been done over the many years of family reunions. The three of them together without spouses showed a change: all the other photos over the years had been of a large group, including spouses.

It was a special day and event for Iva Mae. She was the center of attention, which she loved, plus she was surrounded by her family and friends. Sandy's backyard was full of people, tables, and chairs. The theme was Fourth of July since Iva Mae's birthday was on July 3, and red, white, and blue colors were everywhere. Tables were covered with the theme, and the whole yard had a festive look. The food was plentiful and typical of a family event, including fried chicken, potato salad, and chocolate cake. It had the feeling of the past family reunions when Mary and Lula provided much of the atmosphere and sense of family center. This party had Sandy and Robin's stamp on it, and although it was different from the past, it gave their mother a feeling of old and good times.

Iva Mae spent the entire day visiting with everyone, telling them how surprised she was and how she'd had no idea that Sandy had planned the party. She especially enjoyed her grandchildren, as her relationships with them were so much closer and easier than those with her children. She talked about how she would have dressed up and fixed her hair more if she had known it was her birthday party and so many people were going to be there. The party exhausted her, but she was happy to have so many people come because they liked her. At the end of the day and cleanup, she was sad that it was over, but she treasured the memories of the day for many years, including the conversations about specific family members and stories told from her youth.

Iva Mae was starting to look and act a little older. Her hair had grown in a beautiful white-gray, starting from the front and moving gradually to the back as if she meant for it to be that way. It was more gray than her natural color now. She had always taken pride in taking care of her hair. She kept it short but would get it styled, and later in life added a permanent to give it curl and body, as her hair was naturally straight. She had gained weight again over the years and was having more difficulty walking from lack of exercise, and she was often sick with lung problems and on antibiotics. But no matter the circumstances, they did not stop her from being on the go and continuing to see and do as much as possible.

Chapter 39

The 1990s ushered in the last decade of the century and with it a sense that the world was in the process of massive change. The decade brought the end of the Cold War but the rise of terrorism. The United States was the strongest nation in the world, with a powerful military and economy. The world was at the forefront of becoming digital as the Internet became available for unrestricted commercial use. Throughout the decade, inflation continued to rise, and cellular phone usage was starting to become widespread. The field of science saw major advances during this period that had previously been the stuff of science fiction. The first cloning of an animal and the development and advancement of stem cell research marked the beginning of debates around moral and social issues for years to come.

All the new changes in the world gave Iva Mae more fuel for her predictions that were in the book of Revelation and the apocalypse that was to come. She did not like the way the world was changing. Self-service gas stations had become common with payment at the pump, and Iva Mae did not like anything to do with computers. She did not like or understand banking machines and preferred to work with a person, and anything mechanical confused her and made her nervous, including phone message or automated machines.

Reggie and Amber were in grade school, and Iva Mae's time became freed up outside of taking them to church, school events, and gymnastics as well as dance classes. A friend at her church invited her to join her at a Bible Study Fellowship, or BSF. This was the start of ten years of studying the Bible with a group to learn and understand the scriptures. She was very proud of herself as she worked on her daily lessons and questions. She participated in each class and loved the attention she would receive if she was the only person who had the answer and had actually done the homework.

Around this same time Iva Mae decided to volunteer at the local hospital. A friend of hers told her about a position in the pharmacy where help was needed. Together they worked on the prescription paperwork within the pharmacy, having fun while taking their jobs very seriously. To Iva Mae the work she did for the hospital was exactly what she would tell everyone she knew: work! She would plan her time off so she wouldn't inconvenience anyone or leave the pharmacy shorthanded. She worried that if she was gone on a trip, or ill and could not go to "work," the paperwork would get backed up and then it would be much harder to catch up and complete the task. It was serious business.

Life was going well for Iva Mae. She enjoyed her friends, children, and grandchildren. She kept herself busy with activities. She and Sandy would take quick trips together as well as shop for special occasions. She felt that she had Amber and Reggie on a good road toward being saved through her church influence. Physically, Iva Mae's health was stable for the most part. She still took daily medication for her blood pressure, and occasionally the prescription would need to be changed. This always caused dramatic side effects such as hallucinations, disturbed sleep, and general feelings of lightheadedness. Iva Mae's knees had been giving her problems over the years, and she eventually had to have surgery on one of them. After the surgery her knee was worse, and she had difficulty getting in and out of cars. It did not stop her from traveling, but it was a problem, and she complained continually about the pain. In a short amount of time she had surgery again, and this time it was a knee replacement. This was a very successful procedure and she recovered quickly. She also had begun to have problems with her stomach as well as back pain. Even so, she still looked much younger than her age. Her hair had continued to come in with more white than gray, and it spread from her forehead evenly through her scalp. Through the years her hair continued to turn a beautiful white without a yellow tinge, unlike that of many people her age. Her skin was clear and usually porcelain when she had not spent time in the sun. She had always tanned easily other than the one time she had burned in Florida. She was not a sun worshipper but never took much precaution with her sun care. Overall, her health was a continual issue, but it did not deter Iva Mae from doing the things she wanted to do, and she always looked forward to the next visit from family or trips to see them and the areas where they lived.

It was during this time that Tammy was hired on at the railroad in Springfield. Sandy helped her get this job, and everyone took a deep breath, knowing that she was in a position to earn enough to support herself and Amber. Sandy had an opportunity to transfer to Alabama, and because she had aspirations toward promotions with the railroad, she and Reggie packed up and moved during the early nineties. Tammy and Amber then were transferred to Topeka, Kansas, in the mid-nineties. Iva Mae was relieved that Tammy finally had a good-paying job but worried about her and Amber moving and Tammy's ability to take care of Amber. She was saddened that Sandy and Reggie were moving to Alabama, because she counted on Sandy for so many things, including extra money for helping with Reggie.

Iva Mae's worries with money had continued since moving back to Missouri from Washington. Every year, Denny gave her checks that she could cash monthly to help with her expenses, and each and every year, Iva Mae worried for a month before getting the checks about whether she would have them for the coming year. The apartment she lived in was designated for people with lower incomes, so each year she had to show her income and expenses. Her medical costs were significant, and her prescription medication along with her living expenses took most of her Social Security check each month.

She was an expert at stretching a dollar. She would occasionally splurge and buy something for herself like a new pocketbook, but even then she would find it on sale and have a coupon just for the purchase. She had spent many years watching her budget and had a habit of checking grocery fliers and finding the best prices on food. Leading up to the holidays, Iva Mae would gather all her ingredients for her special cookies and candy gifts by watching the sales for flour, sugar, chocolate, and other items, including the metal tins she packed them in to be shipped. It was a major effort and production to buy, make, and pack the items before the shipping dates for her family and friends. She would complain how it was hard for her to lift the heavy cookware and how her back would bother her from standing. Now in her mid-seventies, she would say each year that this might be the last year she would be able to cook all the goodies she so loved to provide to her dear ones. And each year her children would tell her that it was fine if she stopped and she did not need to buy gifts at all. Still Iva Mae continued, even though it was getting harder with her back, and standing for long periods of time was difficult.

Once Iva Mae's core family had moved away, she counted on her friends more than ever. Her work at the hospital continued to be important to her, as it gave her purpose and socialization. She also was much involved with her church friends and Bible study. Her friend June had continued being her best friend throughout their life, and they talked often on the phone even though they did not see each other as much. She kept busy with going places with her friends, as well as trips with Denny and his new wife, Jane. They had married in the early nineties after meeting and developing a relationship that fit both their lifestyles.

Iva Mae was able to visit Sandy in Alabama and Robin in South Carolina. While in South Carolina, she and Robin went to Charleston for the weekend. This was Iva Mae's first trip to Charleston, and she was fascinated by how old it was, including one of the churches she stopped in where she told everyone how old it smelled. Her other thoughts about Charleston were how it was much like Europe "without a Kmart or Walmart in sight."

An illness during this time period had Iva Mae home for a while. She complained of being sick to her stomach, and heartburn. This continued for several days until a friend convinced her she needed to see a doctor. It turned out to be her heart, and she was immediately put into the hospital to have a stent put in for the artery blockage that had developed. She was scared and her children were worried, but she bounced right back and was given nitroglycerin medication to have with her for future chest pain. The blockage and the procedure affected her physically and mentally, and a dramatic slowdown began to be seen in her character and way of life. She began to attend the rehab program housed at Hammons Heart Institute at the hospital where she volunteered. She had a surprise one day when she arrived at rehab. Her niece's husband, Tim, was at the center for the same purpose of exercising after his heart surgery. He wrote the following recollection:

> What a great lady. I had coronary bypass surgery at St. John's (now Mercy) Hospital. They had and still have a very progressive coronary rehab program housed at Hammons Heart Institute on the hospital campus. Many

of those who complete the post-op rehab program continue to exercise there after completing the initial program. In fact they have a very loyal clientele of mostly senior citizens. I had exercised there for several months when one Saturday morning while I was in the warm-up stretch area, a lady turned to me and said, "Tim, is that you?"

I recognized Iva Mae immediately, and we quickly struck up a conversation. Sally and I hadn't seen Iva Mae in the five or so years since Sally and her brothers had become estranged from their dad, Raymond. Iva Mae told me that she was afraid that Sally was mad at her too. "No, that's not the case at all!" I gladly told her. We chattered for a while, catching up on each other's families. I told Iva Mae that Sally would love to see her. It wasn't long after that that we got together and Sally and Iva Mae rekindled their bond. What a blessing it was to have her. I will always be glad that our chance meeting took place.

Iva Mae felt the same way and loved that Sally and Tim were again part of her life. She felt that her brother was wrong, and never could understand the relationship he did not and could not have with his own children. Raymond had divorced his children's mother and then married a woman whom many in the family did not like or want to be around. She was the type of person who could suck all the good out of a room. Iva Mae was not fond of her brother's second wife but kept her relationship with them both for the sake of Raymond. Having Sally in her life was like having another daughter, and with Sandy gone, she rejoiced that she had family close by just in case she needed them.

As part of her growing relationships, she developed a strong bond with her new friend from her church at South Haven. Vivian and her husband, Tanner, became very close friends with Iva Mae. Vivian and Iva Mae would talk daily on the phone and many times more than once a day. They planned outings and dinners together as well as trips that Vivian and Tanner were organizing through the church. This friendship was special to them both, as Vivian recalled in a note she wrote for one of Iva Mae's birthdays.

> Iva Mae has been a blessing to us in every way. We always needed volunteers, and she has always been available (even if she was busy). She always had a cheerful attitude that encouraged others. She has a God-given talent for being thoughtful. The light that shines from her heart continues to touch all of us. She has graciously allowed me to be her exercise partner at the heart center. Friends who sweat together stay together. Iva Mae's love and pride in her children and grandchildren shows in her speech as well as her actions. The way she shares stories and photos of her family makes you like them and want to get to know them. They say to have a friend you must be a friend. She is truly our dear friend.

Chapter 40

It was during this decade that Debi, who had been adopted after birth, was looking for her birth mother and found Sandy. After she contacted Sandy, they began to talk and correspond by mail. Sandy was curious about Debi's life, and Debi wanted to know how she had come to be an adoption case. The following is a letter from Sandy just after Debi had made contact.

Debi, Here are some snapshots. Everyone is real excited about meeting you and your mom. Thought it might be nice to give you a little info—sometimes it is easier to digest in written form.

As far as the family goes, my mother, Iva Mae Hodge, is seventy-one. Her birthday is July 3. She is pretty healthy but has a lung disease that causes her a lot of problems. But she is still active and a good babysitter.

My brother, Dennis (Denny) Wyant, is fifty, his birthday is October 27. He lives in Silver Springs, Maryland, and is head of the DAV [Disabled American Veterans] offices. He has two sons, Mike and Brian. It took him a while, but I believe he has found his soul mate after three tries. His wife's name is Jane (a nurse). Right now they are looking forward to an early retirement to Florida.

My sister Robin and her husband, Steve, live in Greenville, South Carolina. They do not have children but would love to. Steve works for Lockheed Air Craft and Robin works for the Piedmont newspaper. Robin is the sweet one. She can get riled up but is usually very kind and gentle. They have two Dobermans, Cleo and Caesar.

My sister Tammy is unmarried and has an eleven-year-old girl, Amber. Tammy is the smart one. She probably has a high IQ but falls short on horse sense every so often. We have had a time trying to get her going. She just started working for the Burlington Northern railroad recently, and we have great hopes.

Robin and Tammy are my half-sisters. Mom married when she was nineteen to a man thirty years older than her. My dad died when I was in third grade. They had divorced when I was about three. I barely knew him.

As for myself, I told you on the phone my claim to fame is the awe that I survived. Thirty years in a "coma," better known as the coma years. I find it pretty amazing that I was so unaware of what was going on around me. It was probably a withdrawing effect having to do with bouncing around so much from home to home. When Mom divorced my dad, I lived with relatives. Then she and my stepfather were not real happy. Actually they gave new meaning to the word *poor*. But we all made it.

My whole high school experience was pretty dismal and foggy. I was supposed to go to college, but I couldn't stand it, so I went to work in a factory. Talk about a nightmare. I really hated that job. That is where I worked when I got pregnant. It sure gave the old ladies something to talk about. Remember this was the late 1960s. Anyway it was decided at home that it would be impossible for me to keep a baby. I fought, screamed, cried, and gave in.

I went to Kansas City to a home for unwed mothers and suffered out the summer. Believe me it was hot there. It was in a bad neighborhood. Actually some of it had been burnt out during the race riots the year before. A poor white girl from the Ozark hills was scared.

But here is what I gained from my loss, and I did feel a loss. I don't know if I can describe that, I'm not sure there are words for it. Anyway . . .

I had to take care of myself. You know, laundry and my stuff. I had to fight a few verbal battles with some real scary girls there and found out that I could hold my own. I found out what other girls my age were doing. Some not that different from me and others were extremely different. It was a real experience. At any rate, when I got home, I had decided that the factory wasn't what I wanted to do all my life. So I took a typing course the next year and then started working for the Frisco Railway in January 1970. It was supposed to be until I could figure out what I wanted to do. You know, something great and impressive. But I decided I really liked the work and have stayed with it for the last twenty-four years now. WOW!

I started as a clerk, then worked as a yardmaster, and now as a train dispatcher. When I started, it was mainly a male-dominated craft. Actually it still is, but we are making headway.

Since I never could get a good mate lined up to marry, I decided I really did need to have a child. I had a good job, good salary, good benefits, and felt like I could handle the social pressure, so with the help of a friend in St. Louis, I had Reggie. Probably the one thing (the most important to me) that I gained from losing you is that I do not allow anyone to make my decisions for me now. It has to be my decision, what feels right for me. What an expensive lesson.

I am so happy with what I have found out about you and your family. Your mother sounds wonderful. It will be so nice to hear about your life. You can't have any idea how many times I feared you were in one of the "bad" homes. What a relief. Thanks for calling. Looking forward to seeing you.

—Sandy

As the decade of the nineties was ending, Iva Mae had a life full of friends, volunteer work, family, and travel. She had a new granddaughter in Debi, who lived in the Missouri capital, and was able to attend her wedding with Sandy and Reggie. Iva Mae was not too excited about having another grandchild in her life, as she felt uncomfortable with the idea and with how people would perceive this secret from the past. But she knew that Sandy was happy and she did not want to cross her, so she looked forward to having Debi be a part of her family. She thought that if Debi liked her, she would get attention from this new part of her family.

Iva Mae went to visit friends, relatives, and her children, and although she preferred to travel by car, she was traveling more by plane these days. When possible her family would drive her to see other family members who were still in the Kansas area. Denny had moved to Indianapolis to complete his working years before retiring to Florida, and Robin had moved to Montgomery, Alabama, with her job. Denny's son Brian graduated from college in Maryland in the late nineties, and the entire family flew in for the event. It was a great visit and celebration of life, and Iva Mae loved that she was in the center of it all. As the mother and grandmother, she felt secure that she was loved and her family was all together with her.

During these last years of the decade Iva Mae traveled often to visit with her children. Many of her trips were with Denny and Jane as they searched for the right place to move to in Florida. Often they were joined by Jane's mother, who was the complete opposite of Iva Mae. Jane's family was Jewish, and Iva Mae just could not understand their way of thinking. Although Jane's mother and Iva Mae got along during these trips, Iva Mae did not like having to share the attention. She did not enjoy being with someone who was so different from herself. Iva Mae felt that the two of them had no connection and that the woman didn't like her. She could not make a friendship because of their vast differences in demeanor and faith, but mostly because of her need to have all the attention. Because of these feelings, she was not a good traveling companion, and many times on trips with her children she was moody and demanding.

As Iva Mae aged, her need to talk—and specifically to talk about herself or family members and how their actions affected her—deepened. She needed to talk. She was uncomfortable with silence and filled the void with conversation. Her need for attention and reassurance that she was liked and loved became more intense as she aged. All conversation was about her life, friends, and family. Occasionally she would talk about politics, which would be connected to how it was going to influence her life or how it was part of the predictions in the Bible. Outside of family, her faith in God was the core of her life, and she was more than ever determined to have her family be saved and ensured a place in heaven. Her beliefs, more often than not, were not welcomed, and sometimes she needed to be reminded that her Bible pamphlets were not welcomed or needed either. She would stop when told but knew she was doing what God would want by spreading his word.

Chapter 41

As the world braced itself for the turn of the millennium and a possible electronic meltdown, Iva Mae's family was once again changing. Sandy was transferring with her job and moving to Fort Worth, Texas. Robin and Steve would soon be moving to South Florida, and Denny had retired from his government work to live in Florida, with Jane still working from home and traveling when needed.

During the 2000 presidential campaign between George Bush and Al Gore, Iva Mae said that Al Gore was a "new ager" and would not be a good president because of his new-age beliefs. She had always been on the Democrat side of politics, but Al Gore had been painted to believe in new-age religion according to the teaching of sermons she watched on television. From that day forward she thought he should not be elected. Once President Bush was in office, she disliked him and his politics. Even during the attack on the Trade Center towers and the aftermath, she did not have faith in Bush. The attacks served to show once again how the days were numbered and Jesus would soon be returning for his children.

At seventy-eight, Iva Mae flew to Alabama to spend the Christmas holidays and the last days of the century with Robin and Sandy and grandchildren. Amber was flown in to be a part of the holiday festivities with Sandy and Reggie. This is when Iva Mae began to talk about each trip being her last. Her signs of aging were showing in her speed and stamina. Traveling alone worried her because she was always nervous about missing her flight. She now had someone from the airlines help her with connections but didn't trust them, and with good reason: she had almost missed a flight when they were not paying attention. All this did not stop her from preparing her homemade bread, cookies, and candies beforehand to mail to her children for the holidays. She also prepared her famous cinnamon rolls for Christmas morning to the pleasure of her grandchildren, since it had become a family tradition.

Knowing that Sandy and Robin were moving even farther away from Missouri worried Iva Mae, but she had her friends and relatives close by in case she needed someone quickly. She had been going through more health issues with back problems and her blood pressure. Her heart occasionally gave her trouble, but overall she was still on the go and looking forward to the next trip or event. She continued to work as a volunteer at the hospital and go to her Bible studies weekly. During this time she had met some people who were starting a new church and invited her to visit. Iva Mae was curious about the church, as the people who had invited her were the preacher and his wife. She was excited because it was a new church just starting. The services were held in a building that they rented, so it wasn't in an actual church. The music was new and contemporary and not the hymns Iva Mae was familiar with and used to singing. She loved to sing but could not carry a tune and knew it. She enjoyed music and especially songs that were about her savior.

From the moment she walked into South Creek Church, Iva Mae felt she had found her new purpose. She was greeted by the two pastors with great warmth and friendship. She was washed over with attention and immediately decided this was her new church. She would be one of the founding and eldest members. The church members were young and full of energy like most of her friends throughout her life. Her faith and love for God was once again strengthened, and her purpose to reach and teach as many as possible to point them toward salvation was reinforced.

More trips were planned as the new century started. Iva Mae was now in her late seventies, and each year after her birthday she told people she was almost the next year's age. This continued for the remainder of her life. She would get frustrated as she aged because she looked younger than her years. People did not recognize that she was older, and she didn't think she was getting the respect she was due for her years in regard to all her health and aging issues. Her children had many inside jokes with her about it and who was her favorite child or grandchild of the moment based on what they had done for her. She took most of it in stride as long as she was getting the attention she wanted and needed.

Early in the decade the family was busy with many events that Iva Mae was proud to attend. A trip to Florida to visit Robin included a gambling boat trip for the day. Iva Mae proudly wore her "Jesus Saves" costume diamond pin. A woman on the boat asked her what Jesus would think about her gambling on the slot machines. Iva Mae just laughed and didn't pay attention other than to tell the woman that she knew that she was going to heaven and that she hoped the woman was saved.

Robin and Denny trained to run the Disney Marathon that January. Sandy and Debi trained to complete the half marathon as well. Much of the family gathered in Florida, and everyone stayed on Disney property. Iva Mae was happy to be a part of it, although she made a point of telling everyone how difficult it was, getting old. When they didn't give her the sympathy she was looking for, she went on to say, "You will see! Just wait until you're old and have to wear diapers and have trouble doing things. You will see and say I'm right." She was thrilled that Robin had brought food and coffee supplies so she could have her morning coffee and orange juice to take her medication. She was glad there was transportation so she could be at the finish line to applaud as they crossed the end and received their Disney medals. Afterward, with the help of her friend Vivian, she wrote this story for the hospital newsletter:

Setting & Achieving Goals

Recently as I was watching my family (son, two daughters,

and granddaughter) run in the Disney World 26.2 mile
Marathon in Orlando, Florida, I was struck by how
setting goals and working each day to achieve them had
gotten all of us to this day. My son, Dennis, is legally
blind, my daughters were never athletes, and I was not
very active. The day of the race Dennis had a sinus
infection and his temperature was elevated when he
finished the race. He never considered not running or
giving up. Each one finished the race and received a
medal for the completion within the allowed time. My
children (including spouses) encourage each other and
have a history of setting goals and not quitting till they are
reached. I had a stroke a few years ago, and recently I had
a heart attack. I work out at the Hammonds Heart Center
three times per week following a supervised exercise plan
and have an eating plan. I have been a volunteer (in
Pharmacy at St. John's) for over ten years. There are days
I do not feel like going to exercise or to work at the
hospital, but I set goals for myself. I want to be healthy
and live independently. With the guidance of an exercise
physiologist at Hammons I believe I will be able to live an
active and meaningful life and be there to cheer on my
children as we all work at achieving our goals.

Another trip for Iva Mae was when Amber graduated high
school and the family all gathered in Topeka to attend the
ceremony and have the required family photo taken.

Several months after that trip to Disney World, Denny
surprised everyone with a letter that began, "Like the movie
said, life is like a box of chocolates, you never know what you
are going to get." One summer in the early sixties, Denny had
applied for jobs near Branson, Missouri, and landed a position

in the Rockaway Beach area at the Taneycomo Country Club as the assistant greens keeper by day and waiter at the nightclub in the evenings. During that summer Denny "dated" a local girl one evening, and the consequences of that night returned to him forty years later. He received a call asking if he was the Dennis Wyant who used to work at Rockaway Beach; if so, the woman said, "You are my dad." Denny's daughter, Nancy, had found him, and once she met and began to catch up on a lifetime, she was meeting the family also. Nancy came to the Disney marathon event and became another member of the family. She wanted to be engaged with everyone and learn about their life and background. Growing up in the Kansas City area with wonderful adoptive parents and a brother, also adopted, she had had a great childhood. Nancy was married to a physician and had a child of her own. There was no doubt that she was part of the Wyants; she looked just like them: tall, like the rest, and with the same facial features. Nancy was excited to finally have information about where she came from and how she was similar to these family members.

Nancy remembered her journey to meet her father and grandmother with these thoughts:

> In the year 2000 I had decided that this is the year I would find my birthmother. And if that miracle happened, then I might be brave enough to search for my birthfather. I had no idea if they were alive, if they were receptive to meeting, and if my birthfather's identity was even known. I went through the long, arduous process of searching . . . support groups, juvenile court, networking, and so on. I hired a "searcher" out of Minnesota to make contact with my birth mom, as the only information we were able to collect was hers. She was found and letters were

exchanged through the searcher.

After months, my mother decided she wanted to reveal her name and then we could communicate openly. In the meantime, she did provide my father's name to the searcher. They had no communication after I was conceived, and he apparently never knew I existed. My birthmother sent an article she had found about my father in a book of "Who's Who." My father was an easy find for the searcher because he was prominent in the U.S. government. His name couldn't be released just yet, and the searcher made contact with him after my mom and I met for the first time. The searcher contacted my birthfather, Dennis, and he was curious and receptive. We had our first conversation when I was at a hotel in Memphis, Tennessee, traveling through and he was vacationing in Alaska with his wife, Jane. This was summer 2001. We did DNA testing and met face-to-face when he visited me in Leawood, Kansas, in October of that year.

Once I started communicating with both sides of my family, to my amazement, both of my biological grandmothers were still alive! I had lost both of my grandmothers in my adoptive family years earlier. Pictures starting coming to me from both my birth mom and birth dad of them and family members so I could start to put everyone in place. I don't know exactly when my birth dad told his mother, Iva Mae, that she had another grandchild, but he said she was dismissive. Actually, it was more than dismissive. Downright not interested, and that she didn't need any more grandchildren. Dad's sister Tammy had a child, Amber, with no active father, and

Dad's sister Sandy had a child, Reggie, with no active father, and had given up a baby girl for adoption as well. Grandma Iva Mae already had two grandsons through Dad Dennis whom she helped raise. In the pecking order, I was automatically at the top as being the oldest, as my dad would have been eighteen years old when I was born, and he was the oldest child of Iva Mae's.

Since it has been many years ago that the meetings took place, it's a little fuzzy how it all came together. Maybe it was after Dad showed his mom my letter and photos of me and her great-grandchild, Jillian. Maybe that piqued her interest. I don't remember if we exchanged letters or just picked up the phone and called. Because she was in Springfield, Missouri, and I lived in the Kansas City, Missouri, area, we were only about three hours apart. I had started making frequent trips to Branson, Missouri, where my birthmother lived, to get to know her better, so would be coming right through Springfield. She softened, obviously, or she wouldn't have agreed to meet. I went to her apartment, could smell wonderful food aromas seeping from under the door, knocked, and she opened it! There we were, face-to-face . . . same height, same blue eyes. I couldn't believe I had a grandma as tall as I was! We hugged and she invited me in. We spent time getting to know each other. It was easy, as we both love to talk! We formed a quick relationship and talked about many things.

She sent me a lot of notes, letters, and greeting cards. I found one postmarked July 16, 2001. I sent her photos of me and my family. She said, "Yes, I was surprised to know I had another grandchild and great-grandchild. BUT I am always getting surprises. Ha! As Denny says, Life is a box of chocolates. Nancy, you have a complexion like Mike, Denny, and Denny's Dad, and you favor them. I am five feet nine, but I don't have your figure. Ha! It was so interesting to see these pictures. Denny was a handful when he was young, but he has made me proud and he is so good to me. I love my girls also. The grandchildren are super" . . . then closes with "Really am anxious to see you all. Love, Grandma Iva Mae."

Cards were coming frequently, and I made another trip through town when Sandy, Tammy, and Amber were visiting. I was nervous about that. Amber and Tammy sat on the couch with their arms crossed, just looking me over. Sandy was very welcoming. By the end of the evening, we were having a lot of fun going through photo albums. I received a card several days later that said, "Everyone liked you!" And, "You are always welcome any time." Another card said, "Thank you for coming and taking me to lunch. I love to see you and talk. I enjoyed every minute."

Grandma always looked pretty when going out even for a casual lunch. She looked great for her age, wore stylish clothes, and always made sure she had on her flashy jewelry. She shared many stories of her kids, raising her grandkids, and her travels. She really got around! I had formed an opinion of Grandma from talking to family, and I thought she might be difficult. I never saw that side of her, only the loving, sweet, chatty Iva Mae. I asked her once about some of the men in the complex where she lived, and she quickly said, "Why would I get married again? Just to have an old man sitting around in the house and having to take care of him?" Well said.

I was exposed to her cooking on my very first visit. The red velvet cake sticks out, but we were all so lucky to get boxes of homemade cookies for Christmas, and even better, a cookbook she compiled of her recipes. She also had a collection of decorative plates on her walls that all had brought her from visits all over the world. Each visit, I was told which plates I would get when she was gone. And I did! Oh, and she loved her church family. They treated her like royalty, and I believe she was the oldest in the congregation. We heard more than once about the rapture. She was quite looking forward to it. I hope she wasn't disappointed.

I drove to Springfield and picked her up and brought her to our house in Leawood, Kansas, for a couple of days. We drove through the old areas of Kansas City where she lived and worked as a young woman. She was an easy houseguest, and she even tolerated my cats. She had mentioned more than once that she had a brother who threw farm cats on her when she was little, and she's never liked cats since.

Grandma moved one more time while in Springfield, and I could tell she wasn't happy there. She moved to Fort Worth, Texas, to be closer to her girls, and had a lovely apartment in which she could still do some cooking, but seems like she was happiest being surrounded by family photos, her television, a newspaper, and books. Dad would send her articles on the Springfield, Missouri, college Lady Bears team, which she looked forward to reading about.

She was an interesting lady with many friends. I was honored to attend her eightieth birthday party. We really could sit and talk for hours. She was honest with me and felt she could confide in me, which was easy because she didn't raise me nor was I involved in any family history. We had a very special relationship. I miss her.

Once Iva Mae had met Nancy in Springfield and loved the idea of another member of the family who liked her and paid attention to her, she immediately added Nancy's birthday, anniversary, and other important days to the list she kept in an address book. Each member of the family's special days was acknowledged with a call, card, and gift or gift card. All of Iva Mae's life she sent her grandchildren a few dollar bills in the mail for holidays like Valentine's Day so they would know she was thinking of them. She wanted to make sure each child and grandchild knew that she cared about them. She was not skilled at finding special things that each person would like, but if she did, that would be their gift from her for the rest of her life. Denny and his boys received chocolate chip cookies because it was the only gift she knew they enjoyed. During the years Reggie and Amber were close by, she would get gift ideas from Sandy and Tammy. She didn't enjoy putting gifts together and loved it when gift bags became popular. She would tell family members that she had a sack for the gift. She was teased about her gift wrapping. Any time she wrapped a gift, it would be secured with so much tape that the person opening it would need scissors or a knife to get in. Packages for mail were consumed in packing tape so she didn't have to worry they would open in the shipping. Anytime a package or gift had extra tape on it, everyone knew who had wrapped it, and Iva Mae took the teasing in good spirits.

Iva Mae had a sense of humor. Her friends loved her laugh and her humor. Her family was not as comfortable with it. For some unknown reason Iva Mae had a need to point out her children's most embarrassing moments to others, many times to strangers, as a funny thought or situation. She was not a private person, although there were many times in her life that she did not talk about or that she would gloss over without a lot of details. For the most part she lived in the moment rather than the past and would say that she had done the best she could. Her future was important mainly for her security and the afterlife. As she grew older, she worried about her children, but rarely did she ask for details about their lives; she focused more on their connection with her.

Oddly, Iva Mae did not have many thoughts on the tragedy of September 11 that year other than saying she felt terrible for the people who had to endure the experience. It also confirmed that the end of the world was at hand just like the Bible predicted, and that the Second Coming would be any day. She knew it was true and made sure everyone she talked to knew it and was preparing.

Chapter 42

In 2002 Iva Mae was turning eighty. The family decided it was time to have a celebration for her to mark this special birthday. The plan was to have as many family members as possible come together in Springfield for a three-day celebration that included a large birthday party.

The first event was planned for Friday evening. Iva Mae's children and grandchildren along with a few of their cousins all met for dinner at the W&W Café in Hurley, Missouri. Fried chicken and to-die-for pies were on the menu and enjoyed by all. Everyone took pleasure going back in time to see old friends and places where they had lived while celebrating their time together. Iva Mae was delighted to have all her family with her but as always just wanted a little more attention. Tammy commented that it would never be enough. She said, "Mom could have all her children and grandchildren sitting at her feet just waiting to listen to her, and it still would not be enough for her." Iva Mae loved the attention, but she always wanted more. By now she had four children, six grandchildren, and three great-grandchildren—one from Nancy and two from Debi.

The second day of her celebration was a huge party at the local senior center that the family rented for the day. Invitations were sent out in the mail and by word of mouth that all were invited. Iva Mae's grandchildren were keeping her entertained that morning while everyone hurried to prepare the place for the party. Once she arrived, she was surprised because she hadn't known what was in store for her. Guests started arriving at noon, and over two hundred family, friends, and acquaintances came to pay tribute to her. She was delighted as she was showered with gifts, compliments, and cards. For years, cards celebrating her birthday and holidays had been a big deal to her. She counted how many cards she received and reported the number to her children each time. It became another joke to everyone, and they often asked her how many cards she had received for any given occasion.

The party was a big reunion of family members but also of old friends, many of whom had not seen each other for many years. The day was extremely successful other than Iva Mae being disappointed that she did not get to spend enough time talking to each person and her visits with people were too short.

After the party and cleanup, the family took the leftover food to the hotel for dinner snacks and spent the rest of the evening visiting and enjoying time together. Iva Mae was staying at the hotel with the family so she wouldn't feel left out. It was a wonderful time for her. The next morning those who could went to breakfast at Hemingway's on the patio at the Bass Pro shop. It was a large crowd and everyone talked nonstop, which made Iva Mae very happy. It was over too soon as far as Iva Mae was concerned, and she said so as she gave her goodbyes and began to tell everyone she was almost eighty-one.

Once the big party was over, Iva Mae's next trip was in the planning. Sandy was transferred to Redlands, California, and Iva Mae left that August and flew into Ontario International Airport, going through Dallas.

Had a good flight and I dreaded Dallas–Fort Worth, but everything went perfect. I had a good seat companion from Dallas. Sandy met me and we went to a good restaurant where I had the best clam chowder. We then drove all around Redlands where Sandy showed me everything. There is a tree here that will mist on you when you stand under it, and I get sprinkled every day. The following day Sandy had to work but I enjoyed the day reading. Snowball, Sandy's Westminster terrier, loved the bone I brought him and he seems to enjoy having me here. When Sandy got home, we went to the Redlands farmers market. We ate corn on the cob right on the street, and then we drove around and saw the hills that surround the area. Now I know where the western films were made before the roads were here.

Sandy had to work again the following day so Snowball and I played around and rested. When she got home, we went to the mall and you know what that called for—a sale! I bought two tops, and then we went to the Redlands Bowl and there was entertainment. It was good with bagpipes, violin, and cello.

The next day we went to Los Angeles and Hollywood to another farmers market and they had the best fruit. Hollywood was crowded. We took a ride on the trolley and saw a lot. We went to the Chinese Theater to see all the foot- and hand-prints of the actors. Sandy got a kick out of Jeanette McDonald's feel. They were so small. On the way home we stopped at a shoe store to shop after seeing all those footprints!

We couldn't find Nathan's for a hot dog, but someone told us about Pinks. We went there and it was a forty-minute wait in line. I got a Polish with sauerkraut and lemonade to drink. Pinks has been at that location since 1939. Many movie stars have been there and the walls were lined with photos. Afterward we went to the Hollywood Bowl, then to see the Hollywood sign.

On Sunday, we went to Los Angeles and Hollywood again. The first stop was to the La Brea Tar Pits. They are very unusual. Then we went to the Wyndham Bel Age Hotel to church services. Della Reese is the pastor and she was there. It was two hours long. Afterward we were at the House of Blues for a brunch. They had a stage show, and then we drove to Sunset Boulevard and

Beverly Hills. After that we were back in Redlands, and Sandy showed me where she works and I met some of her coworkers.

Monday we went to an outlet mall towards Palm Springs. It was Desert Hills outlet mall and it was fun seeing the desert and hills. On the way home we came by the mountains and into an apple orchard. We stopped at Oak Glen at Apple Dumpling's restaurant. We ordered one apple dumpling and divided it between us, as it was huge. I got a surprise call from Vivian that evening and told her all about my trip so far.

On Tuesday we went to Catalina Island. We started out at seven thirty in the morning and the traffic was terrible. We drove to Long Beach, then took a boat to the island. There was probably around three hundred on the boat going out to the island. When we got to the island it was lunchtime, then we took a tour. The roads are crooked and hilly. You can't take a car on the island so they have golf carts and bicycles. It was interesting and reminded me of the Greek islands. They also have flying fish here. We were tired when we got home tonight. Anyway, I was.

Wednesday we didn't get a start until around noon. I washed two loads of clothes and did some pressing before we went. First we stopped at the Redlands depot that had been made over. We had lunch there, and it was real nice and busy. Afterward we left for Palm Springs. We drove the mountain road to San Bernardino National Forest, and it was all mountains and rocks. Glad Sandy was the driver. We were about five thousand feet up most of the time. Then we hit the Santa Rosa and San Jacinto

mountains. It was beautiful and different. When we hit
Palm Springs, we drove around, then went on the Palm
Spring aerial tram. It was a WOW, as they say. We went
up two and one half miles to eighty-five hundred feet.
When we got up there, we had dinner. Looked around
and took some pictures. Once we came down, we headed
to the highway and home. It was thrilling!

The following day we headed to Dean (Lula's son) and
Carol's. They live in Laguna Hills. It is near the Pacific
Ocean. We got up there and went to eat lunch before we
went to Dean's. They have a beautiful home. Carol and I
talked and talked. When Mitch and Dean got home, we
went to eat at Dana Point Wharf. It is on the ocean and
we watched the sailboats while we ate. I had salmon.
Then Sandy went home and I stayed to visit. We talked
and caught up until bedtime.

The next morning I got up and Dean was downstairs so
we drank coffee and talked till the rest of the house got
up. We then went for a ride along the ocean. We stopped
at an antique shop, then ate lunch. They pointed things
out to me as we drove. The rich people live up here. I just
love Carol and Dean's home. It is really beautiful and has
a pool. I heard that President Bush was visiting not far
from us.

The next morning we were all lazy. Dean got us breakfast
and it was really good. We had French toast, bacon,
orange juice, and coffee. We then went over to Jill's, their
daughter's, home. We went shopping a little, and while
Mitch and Dean watched football, we talked. We are a
talking bunch!

Sunday morning we got up early because we were going to Mike's church, which is eighty-six miles away in the desert at Victorville. There are lots of Joshua trees to see on the way there. We had the best times. Mike, Dean's son, is a preacher. I loved his wife, and the kids were so nice. They had us all for lunch, and then Sandy came up also so I could go home with her. It was one of my best days.

I spent the next day packing and washing at Sandy's, getting ready to go home. Sandy had to go back to work today and when she gets off, we are going out to eat and to a movie. We went to see *Road to Perdition*. It was good. We also ate at a fish place that I enjoyed.

It's Tuesday and time to go home. I got home at seven o'clock and what a day. We got up at four thirty this morning and went to the airport. Everything was fine till I got to Dallas. I missed my plane and had to wait for the next one. Poor Vivian and Tanner were waiting on me. What good friends they are and acted like it was super and they had fun waiting!

I went to bed at nine and didn't get up till seven the next morning and didn't even go to the bathroom in the middle of the night!

Iva Mae 80th birthday

Chapter 43

B y the time Iva Mae had entered her eighties, the world was becoming digital and email was the way the family had contact much of the time. Iva Mae refused to have anything to do with computers and did not want to learn anything about them or to touch them. She was upset that she was missing out on conversations that went on between her children, and her grandchildren were not very good at writing notes to her, including thank-you letters. She still didn't budge on the computer, even when Sandy offered to get her an email-only device. She was adamant. So Denny found a company that would accept emails and print them as letters and mail them to the recipient for a monthly fee. The family was encouraged to email Iva Mae. She loved getting the notes and felt involved and not left out of the digital age.

In 2003, at eighty-one, Iva Mae was going on a cruise ship for the first time. Her son, Denny, was turning sixty, and along with having a party in Florida, the family and some friends were taking a cruise to the Bahamas over a weekend. Iva Mae was happy to be able to go on the trip and see a cruise ship but even more to be able to visit with her children and grandchildren as well as see the ocean on a big cruise ship. Although she had been on a big ship in the Greek Islands, this was totally different. She was beginning to show signs of frailty, but she didn't rest any more than she had to, as she did not want to miss out on anything her family was doing. She loved being the head of the family and the attention she received from the crew of the ship, especially from the waiter during dinner. With help from Sandy she made it around the ship to different shows and the pool, and she enjoyed the sightseeing in Nassau and the contrast in living conditions. But her favorite part was being able to spend time talking and getting attention from her grandchildren and being a part of the group.

Her next trip was to Topeka to attend her granddaughter Amber's wedding. Amber was getting married to Michael in a lovely outdoor wedding, and Iva Mae was not going to miss the event. Unfortunately other family members were unable to attend, so Iva Mae and her daughter Tammy were the only ones in attendance from Amber's side of the family. Iva Mae was proud to be there, especially since it was her granddaughter and she could brag to anyone who listened how she was the person who had watched her and taken care of her when she was young. She worried and hoped that Amber was going to be okay, as she didn't have much faith in marriage and men in general. Tammy and Iva Mae got along well that day, which may have been more for Amber's sake since their relationship had been strained for some time now.

In September of that year, Amber gave birth to Robyn, and Iva Mae was excited to have another great-grandchild. She couldn't wait to see her, and as soon as possible, Robin flew in from Florida and drove her mother to Topeka to visit. Iva Mae loved babies. She told her children often that she had no interest in being in a nursing home and having someone visit with a dog. She would much rather hold a baby. Of course her two biggest fears in life were losing her mind and not knowing who she was or what she was doing, and being put into a nursing home. These fears bothered her often, and her children reassured her that if she did become unable to remember or know who she was, she would not know and her kids would take care of her.

Reggie had begun to work with the railroad by 2002 and worked in and traveled to Oregon, Memphis, and Los Angeles. Sandy was happy to have him close by, and when she moved back to Texas with a transfer in 2005, Reggie soon followed and purchased a home not far from his mother's house. It wasn't long after that that Tammy moved to Fort Worth as well and was living with Sandy once more.

Iva Mae's back continued to give her problems, and her physicians recommended back surgery. She had quit going to the hospital gym for exercise when she had stopped her volunteer work. She had walked the halls of her apartment complex for exercise for some time, but even that had become too painful. Her health had continued to give her problems. She had bunions, and her feet hurt. She still needed antibiotics almost monthly for her lung disease, and she had an oxygen machine in her bedroom to use at night to help her breathing. Her blood pressure medication had continued to change over the years, and her other prescriptions included medicine for acid reflux, water pills, and ibuprofen. Now she also carried nitroglycerin pills that she needed occasionally for her heart. Her weight was around two hundred pounds, but because she got very little exercise, she was soft and had very little muscle tone. She had difficulty getting in and out of chairs, and on one visit she and Robin looked into recliners with motors to help lift you up and make it easier to get out of the chair. Iva Mae's Medicare plan helped with the purchase, and she had the chair for many years.

Over the past few years she had become unhappy with the management at her apartment complex. She had started to become afraid of some of the new people living there and felt that it was no longer safe. During this period she somehow became scared that she was not going to be able to continue living her current lifestyle and began to look for an alternative situation for after the surgery. She found a very-low-income, assisted-living complex in Springfield where she could have a one-bedroom and bath apartment much like a dorm room with a cafeteria for meals. She decided she was going to move there, sell her car, and not drive any longer. It's not known if something happened to cause this major decision, as she did not consult with her family as usual but moved forward as if this were her only choice.

The building was old, and many of the people living in the complex had mental, alcohol, and drug problems. Her apartment consisted of one large room with a bathroom and closet. It had a small refrigerator and cabinet for a few items in the large room. Robin, Amber, and Amber's husband, Michael, came to town to help her with the move. She had a moving company come to handle the big items, and everyone else worked on the rest to save money. The room was set up with her bed and easy chair. She did not have any room for a table. Robin ran around town looking for a large carpet to put over the bare wood floor. She helped her arrange the furniture, unpack her items, and decorate the best she could. Iva Mae was exhausted from the move, and Robin was upset and frustrated.

Everyone was shocked by the decision and didn't quite understand the motive behind it. Other family members came to visit. Once when Nancy was there, she and Iva Mae went to get into the elevator and found someone passed out on the floor from either drinking or drugs. Iva Mae would talk about the conditions of the place with her friends and report to her family that her friends did not understand why her children let her live in those conditions. Her family was confused and frustrated by the whole situation. Once moved in, Iva Mae went forward with the surgery and Sandy came to be with her during that time. It was not an easy surgery at her age and in her state of health. She had a difficult recovery, and Sandy could see that she was not in a good place or in good health, so she began the search for a place for Iva Mae in Texas.

ROBIN ANNE GRIFFITHS

Chapter 44

S andy found a few low-income senior living apartments
and one in particular that seemed to be the best. It was
part of the largest national Jewish-sponsored federally
subsidized housing program for the elderly in the United States
and twenty-five miles from where Sandy lived. The apartment
was in a high-rise senior apartment complex with an active
senior group. They had a pancake breakfast each month, plus
special events and other group activities. Iva Mae agreed to the

move but had great reservations because it was so far away from Sandy. In 2006, with Reggie's help, Sandy went to Springfield to get her mother packed and moved into the new apartment. The complex was clean, with good lighting, and well kept. The community had a library, laundry facilities, and a patio area with a gazebo, including outdoor seating areas. Many of the residents would spend time down in the lobby area visiting each other.

Iva Mae's apartment was on the third floor. It had a small kitchen, one bedroom, and a bathroom. It was roomy enough and comfortable. The living area had a large picture window with a beautiful, large tree just outside. The colors from the different seasons gave Iva Mae a lovely view all year long, although she never really appreciated the beauty in nature or the squirrels and birds that gave her little shows throughout the year. Sandy helped get everything moved in and found a futon sofa that would serve as a guest bed for company. They hung many of her collected plates on the walls as well as family photos, and decorated with crafty touches that Sandy provided. Sandy then got her mother set up with public assistance and new doctors, and was able to cut her medical and drug expenses immensely.

Iva Mae was happy to be closer to Sandy but missed her friends and church in Springfield. Sandy took her mother to several churches in the area, but Iva Mae was not happy with any of them and decided to get all her services from television on Sunday mornings. She was also not interested in making friends at the facility, because she thought they were all Russian Jews and that she did not have anything in common with them. She told her family that she did not understand them with their accents and could not talk to them, because her beliefs were so different. Sandy tried to encourage her to get involved with the book club, but she did not like the books they were reading. She also refused to do any volunteering, telling anyone who asked that she had served her time "working" and was not interested in doing any more. She continued to cook special dinners to celebrate birthdays for Sandy, Reggie, Tammy, and Amber, and she continued her Christmas candy and cookie-baking traditions. At this point in her life it took her much longer to do the cooking, and she needed to sit on a stool in the kitchen part of the time as she fixed her ingredients and baked.

Iva Mae's favorite thing to do was to go out shopping with Sandy, including going to a restaurant for a meal. She counted on Sandy for everything and worried that she would miss something if Sandy didn't take care of it or plan for it. Sandy and Tammy were taking her grocery shopping, to movies, and to doctor appointments, and doing anything else she needed to have done. Sandy took the brunt of the responsibility since Tammy and Iva Mae still had many difficulties getting along. Iva Mae was beginning to be a little picky about where they ate, and she most often did not enjoy the movies because she said they had become too graphic or the language upset her.

When Sandy asked her where she wanted to go to eat, her mother would respond that she did not care except she did not want Mexican food or deli. Sandy would continue to name different food venues and her mother would decline each until she would end with "But I am fine with anything." She took the opportunity whenever she was with Tammy to express how she worried about her, Amber, and Amber's children because they were not going to church. Amber had her second child, Gabrial (Gabe), in May 2006.

When shopping, Iva Mae was having a difficult time going far or sometimes keeping her balance while walking. She used a shopping cart almost as a walker to help her feel more confident. She refused to use a motorized shopping cart even though walking was sometimes exhausting for her. Her excuse was that people would think she was old, but family members believed she was intimidated by the technology and was afraid she would not be able to drive it or would have an accident.

She complained often about not feeling well and about how she would just run out of energy. Each time she began to feel ill, she would tell her children how getting old was not fun and she was ready to be called to God. She was ready and willing to go. Although she would say it with conviction, she would then be afraid when a storm was in the area. She was especially afraid of tornadoes and also found them inconvenient, since she would have to leave her apartment to go to safety on the first floor of the building. She did not drink enough water, which affected her health and even put her in the emergency room a few times. After receiving a phone call, Sandy would spend considerable time in the waiting room while her mother was being seen and treated. Sandy would talk to her about what she was eating and drinking to make sure she was getting the right nutrition. Her mother would tell her that she had hardly eaten a thing and then go on to say that she had had only an orange, a piece of toast, and other items—more than enough, although not often healthful choices. Iva Mae complained often that her stomach bothered her and felt swollen. She talked to her doctors about it, and they often checked on it, including administering tests that revealed an ongoing hiatal hernia issue. For most of her life she had eaten too much at a time, and many times she went to the restroom in a restaurant to throw up. Iva Mae had no problem announcing to her daughters that she had to go "stick her finger down her throat and urp" to feel better.

Iva Mae did not miss driving in the least. She was perfectly happy to have others drive her to destinations. She was relieved that others were taking care of paperwork and whatever else needed to be handled, as she did not feel well most of the time and really had no interest in it. She did not like dealing with anything electronically and would call Reggie whenever she became confused about her television cable service or wanted to play a video. She only knew how to retrieve messages on her phone's answering machine, and had Sandy put the voice message that answered on it for her.

The family now was coming to Texas, since Iva Mae had difficulty traveling. Her children came to Fort Worth to visit around her birthday, and although various family members flew or drove in to see her at different times, the big family events were at the end of October around Denny's, Mike's, and Tammy's birthdays, which were one day after the other. These events would be coordinated by Sandy, who would plan entertainment with family outings and host at least one meal at her home. Since Iva Mae could not have everyone at her apartment, she would bake her famous chocolate chip cookies and usually a dessert for dinner that Sandy would have planned. Iva Mae loved the attention from having her children, grandchildren, and great-grandchildren around her. During these events the family would rent a large van to accommodate most of them in getting from one place to the other. The trips to the Fort Worth Stockyards or to Dealey Plaza and the Sixth Floor Museum gave everyone something to do. Sandy had begun to rent a wheelchair for the extra activity that Iva Mae was not used to, and although Iva Mae would make a fuss about it, she would use the chair and in her heart loved that her family was giving her this special attention.

With very little exercise, Iva Mae was becoming soft and losing much of her strength and muscle tone. Robin was shocked on one trip to see her how soft and aged she was becoming. She was staying with her for a few days once when in the middle of the night Iva Mae got up to go to the bathroom. She fell, waking Robin up. Robin rushed in to find her mother on the bathroom floor. She couldn't get herself up. Robin worked to get her sitting up and then helped her onto her knees. It took some time before they got her standing again, and it really shook Robin to know her mother might have been stuck on the floor needing help if she had not been there.

Iva Mae was embarrassed but nonetheless made a joke out of it. She explained that she occasionally had problems with dizziness when she got up and needed to sit on the side of the bed before rising. Her lungs were bothering her more often, and she was on antibiotics almost monthly. She would tell her children in great detail about the phlegm she would cough up, and if possible she would show it to them. More than once she would talk about a relative who had coughed up a stone and then tell her children how she thought he had the same thing she did. Her blood pressure medication had been changed, which produced nightmares and other dreams. Iva Mae would tell Sandy and Tammy about her dreams being so real, with people from the past such as her sisters visiting her as well as others in her apartment who did not belong there. She would talk about the details of the dreams as if they were real, and everyone was beginning to worry and wonder if she was getting to the end of her life now that she was in her mid-eighties.

To help Iva Mae as much as possible, Sandy found someone to stop by every other week to clean her small apartment and do laundry. However, Iva Mae did not want anyone else to do her laundry, so Sandy took on that responsibility as well. Cindy, who was cleaning for Iva Mae, was fast becoming Iva Mae's new friend and person to talk and tell all her stories to. She would brag to her daughters about how much Cindy was doing for her and how thoughtful she was as well as what a good friend she was. These conversations also included comments about how her friends knew how lonely she was and that some had told her she could move back to Springfield and live with them. Sandy was irritated by these remarks because she felt that they were digs that she was not doing enough. It was very hurtful to Sandy and Tammy how their mother was never satisfied. If asked, she would say she was fine or happy, but the conversations always led her daughters to believe she was not happy. One Christmas, Sandy had the celebration at her home with Reggie, Tammy, and Iva Mae. Iva Mae had made a few items for the dinner, and once the gifts were open and the large dinner was eaten, Sandy was cleaning up the kitchen when her mother said, "Well, next year will be better."

Iva Mae's time in her apartment was spent reading, watching television, and talking on the phone to either her friends from Springfield or her children and grandchildren. Denny called on a regular basis and Robin called about every other week, although Iva Mae would get hurt that Robin was not calling her enough and often complained to Sandy about it. She spent most of her time on the phone with Robin saying she wished Robin was more like the others and called more often.

The apartment complex had a security system so that once you entered the building, you had to call the person you were visiting to have them unlock the next door. Most often when Sandy would arrive, Iva Mae would be on the phone. She refused to have call waiting, so Sandy would have to call over and over to see if she was off the phone in order to get into the building. It was annoying to Sandy, but the other residents who hung out in the lobby began to recognize her and let her into the building. Sandy would make conversation with them, and as time passed, the residents would just open the door when they saw her coming. About this time Sandy purchased a mobile phone for her mother, thinking that it might be handy if Iva Mae had a problem when she was in the bathroom or other area of the apartment. As a bonus, she would be able to answer the phone if she was talking on her landline and Sandy needed to get a hold of her. Iva Mae resisted the new technology but learned how to answer the device when Sandy pushed for her to learn.

Chapter 45

As the years progressed, Iva Mae became increasingly glued to the news, and with each report had ways to connect it with the end of the world and the Second Coming, as she liked to remind everyone. Each storm, disaster, report about the rising cost of living, and other national news was cause for conversation about how it was not going to be long until Jesus came back for his children. The signs were there, and she was ready.

One of her last trips on an airline came in 2007 when the family gathered in Boston for Brian's marriage to Alison. Sandy planned the trip the best she could in order for her mother to be as comfortable as possible. It was not easy, as Iva Mae did not like leaving the comfort of her surroundings. She had difficulty with incontinence and often wore an adult diaper. Even with the complexity, she would not have missed the trip, as it was an important day for her as the grandmother to be present and part of the wedding. She looked forward to being escorted down the aisle of the church to be seated in the front representing the family. She loved the attention.

The trip was tiring, with a rehearsal dinner the evening before, the city tour on the duck boat the day of, the trip to the church in the limousine, the ceremony, the reception, and the dinner and celebration. It was a beautiful wedding and perfect in every way. Iva Mae enjoyed each and every part of the event and loved the attention she received from her family. She was exhausted that evening after the dinner but did not want to leave as the party as it was just getting started. She was afraid she'd miss out on something important or an opportunity to be a part of the party. But it was loud, and the attention was turned to the wedding couple and their friends. Sandy took her to her room to get her settled in for the night. The next day the family gathered for breakfast before leaving for different parts of the country. Iva Mae enjoyed the morning. The event was a special one, and for many years afterward, she talked about the attention she had received from her grandchildren and how much they loved her.

Later that year, Sandy, Reggie, Robin, and Steve left for Africa to climb Mount Kilimanjaro. They had been planning the trip for over a year. Iva Mae was distraught with worry that something would happen to Sandy and worried that she wouldn't have anyone to help her. Tammy was infuriated by these comments. She didn't want to take care of her mother as it was, but to be considered unworthy of it was more than she could bear. Tammy was becoming increasingly resentful of her mother. She was having health issues of her own, and between her weight, her diabetes, and her medications, her well-being was declining as well as her patience and tolerance. Iva Mae just did not understand her daughter at all, and their conversations were defensive and adversarial from Tammy's side.

In 2009 Sandy finally retired from her railroad job. She had been looking forward to the day for over thirty years and planned to travel and work on her many craft hobbies. Over the years Sandy took any opportunity to visit her daughter, Debi, and the grandchildren that came over the years. Grant, her first grandson, was now twelve, Emma was nine, and Leo was five. Sandy enjoyed going on trips with and discovering similar traits that she shared with them. She and her longtime friend Donnie decided to marry, which concerned Iva Mae greatly. She was worried that she would lose Sandy's help and attention. She also did not like the idea that Sandy planned to go away for a while after her retirement date. Sandy had arranged for Tammy and Reggie to help Iva Mae while she went on a sabbatical retreat at Flagler Beach in Florida. Once again Iva Mae thought the world would end without Sandy there to take care of all her needs. Sandy spent several months at the beach and exploring the surrounding areas while writing, reading, and making friends locally. She kept in touch with her mother and everyone else but took this time to really focus and treat herself. Iva Mae just did not understand the purpose of this time away and was not happy with the inconvenience that it caused her. She did not dare say anything directly to Sandy for fear it would make her angry, but she certainly let her friends and other family members know that she needed Sandy and would be happy when she returned.

Robin had been going through many personal problems and issues with her own life and finally told her mother that she was getting divorced. Iva Mae took the news without asking many questions other than how the change might affect her life and when Robin would be able to visit her. The conversation was an accumulation of Robin not being able to talk to her mother about personal or emotional details over her lifetime.

The following year, Tammy was turning fifty, and Sandy planned for the family to come to Texas to celebrate her birthday. Tammy's health was continually declining from complications from her diabetes and other medical issues. She was sick often and had problems with the management at her job. She was not an easy person for the family, and she felt the same about them. She marched to a different drummer and had for as long as anyone could remember. During the time leading up to the family event, Sandy had a talk with Tammy, trying to negotiate a way for everyone to just get along rather than have arguments or other confrontations. Tammy took great offense and was very hurt.

The family all came into Fort Worth. During this long weekend celebration Robin, Sandy, and Tammy all went to get tattoos in honor of Tammy's big day. Tammy got her first one—the one she had said she would get over the years. It was her astrological sign of the scorpion. She had it put on her butt with the words *Bite Me*, because, she said, "When I go to the nursing home in diapers and cannot take care of myself, I will be able to tell them all how I feel without saying a word."

The birthday celebrations—Tammy's fiftieth, Michael's fortieth, and Denny's sixty-seventh—went smoothly, and Iva Mae loved being around her children. She had a really special relationship with her grandchildren and them with her. She was different for those she did not count on for anything but love and friendship. But for the people in her life she counted on to take care of her and provide for her, she would push, complain, and use guilt if necessary to get her point across and achieve what she wanted and needed. Tammy once again repeated to her sisters that she felt her mother could have all her children, grandchildren, and great-grandchildren sitting around her feet listening to her every word and it still would not be enough for her. She would need more.

Tammy was still upset and hurt by Sandy's talk, and once the event was over, she decided to move out of Sandy's home. She made the move and during this shift decided to cut the family off and not talk to any of them. She also decided that she did not want to help with her mother's care any longer and the burden was then all Sandy's, although Sandy had been carrying the majority of it up to this point anyway. After Tammy had settled into an apartment, her daughter, Amber, and her family decided to move to Fort Worth to be with her. Once moved, they began to work on building a home where they could all live together.

The next big event after the birthday celebrations was Denny's oldest son, Michael, getting married in Thailand to a beautiful woman, Hrang, from that country. A family trip was planned to attend the wedding, with side trips to Cambodia and

Vietnam. Of course Iva Mae was not going to be able to attend; although she wanted to go, she knew she was unable to make such a big, long trip. Sandy and Reggie were attending as well as Denny, Jane, and Michael's mother, Judy. Once again Iva Mae was worried that both Sandy and Reggie were going to be gone and wondered who she could count on. Tammy was not speaking to anyone, so Sandy made arrangements for the two weeks that she would be gone for her mother to have what she needed. Robin called her often to check in, and the world did not fall apart as Iva Mae had thought it would.

Chapter 46

In 2011, Brian and Alison, with Iva Mae's great-granddaughter Maeve, came to visit her in Texas. One of Iva Mae's greatest delights was holding a baby. During the visit she gave Maeve her first Nilla Wafer. Brian and Alison weren't so sure she should have a second one, but Iva Mae said, "Babies like to have one for each hand!" Maeve beamed with joy over her cookies, and took her first steps straight to her great-grandma. Iva Mae was so proud, and told everyone that Maeve had been named after her, as she thought the name reflected a mixture of her two names.

During that visit Iva Mae told Sandy that Brian had asked her why she had left Washington, DC, those many years ago when she was living with and taking care of them. Iva Mae said that she told Brian that it was because she had a disagreement with his mother about her lifestyle as well as her concern for Mike since he was sneaking out of the house. Iva Mae didn't like that her grandchildren were not being cared for in the manner that she thought they should be at that time.

It was during this time that Donnie and Sandy took a weekend trip. Donnie remembers the story:

> I was in Fort Worth the week of June 20, 2011, and we were going to the Mustang Motorcycle Nationals later in the week, which is historically held in Texas each year. That year it was in Paris, Texas, which is in the northeastern part of the state. Sandy asked if I cared if she drove her car to Paris and just met me there after lunch. That way she could hit the craft shops on the way and I could go directly to the meet. Seemed like a good plan to me, and I told her no problem. The day of the accident was Wednesday, June 22, 2011, around two thirty in the afternoon, give or take a bit. Sandy was traveling east on US Highway 82 between Sherman and Paris. It's a pretty fast road—two lanes, but I recall that the speed limit was seventy. There were rolling hills and a few curves from time to time. Not a bad road at all. From all accounts she was following a tractor trailer and she struck the rear of the trailer as the driver slowed and was turning left onto Tiger Town Road. The truck driver was looking back with

the mirror and saw her hit the corner of the trailer. He got out, and by the time he ran back, Sandy had gotten out of the car and was walking around wanting to know if she had hurt anyone.

An ambulance was called, and she was transported to the hospital in Paris. Before she left the scene, I got a call from her saying, "I got this problem. I've had an accident and I'm okay, but they're taking me to the hospital. Can you pick me up there and we can go check on the car?" At that point I didn't know what was going on. When I got to the hospital, she was in the emergency room and it was apparent that she wasn't going to check on the car. She was admitted with broken ribs. The next day I went and got all of her belongings out of the car. I noted that the speedometer was stuck around fifty-nine miles per hour, just a needle width shy of sixty. It's normal for this to happen on impact. So she wasn't speeding and she had no recollection of the truck ahead. She told me that the last thing she remembered seeing was a car with kids in it. She was so relieved that they were not involved. It appeared that she had dozed off. I knew that at one point she was taking a medication to help her stay awake, but I don't know if she was using it on this day. She had indicated to me that she took it when on long road trips.

When Iva Mae heard about the accident, she told Sandy that she knew exactly how she felt because of the car accident many years earlier on that Missouri highway when she had run into the back of the car full of bricks. She also told Sandy that she was lucky she didn't break as many ribs as she herself had broken in that accident. Iva Mae added that her additional injuries had to have been much more painful than Sandy's.

Sandy just shook her head and agreed that her mother's injuries must have been more horrific.

Sandy began to recover, but it was slow, and although the physicians said she was healing, she just didn't seem to be recovering the way she should. Although she had had problems over the years with her health, she had continued to go and do the things she wanted to do. Sandy began to just focus on the day to day and getting done what she had to do. She had always enjoyed crafting, and now she spent much of her time making jewelry and other fun things when she wasn't taking care of her mother.

During this time, Tammy opened up to the family again, although she was guarded. Amber and her children had begun to spend time with Sandy doing crafts and other fun recreational-type events. Robyn and Gabe looked at Sandy as more of a grandmother figure, since their time with Iva Mae was limited. Neither Tammy nor Amber was comfortable with how Iva Mae would talk to the children about God, heaven, and hell. Her words were frightening as well as critical about how the children were being raised. It was unfortunate, because the children were well behaved and the relationship could have benefited all concerned.

The following year Iva Mae fell and broke her hip. In most cases such a fall would not have caused an injury, but Iva Mae was getting frail and her bones were brittle. As usual Sandy was able to get her the care she needed, but this meant a big change in her mobility. She spent a few weeks in a rehabilitation facility where the doctors and staff emphasized the importance of her therapy and trying to walk. Although she loved the attention the staff gave her while she was in the hospital and rehabilitation center, she complained often of the pain and how hard it was for her. Iva Mae did not always follow the doctor's orders because she thought she knew better. She heard what she wanted to hear from anyone who gave her advice or directions. Iva Mae's body just did not have the strength to lift her weight up easily, and that was that, as far as she was concerned.

Because of Iva Mae's limited movement and ability, Sandy looked for an assisted-living facility for her. Iva Mae was not keen on the idea of moving, especially to anything that sounded close to a nursing home. All her life Iva Mae's fears of not having money along with losing her memory was wrapped around and included being put into a nursing home. Sandy found a suitable place, and once she took her mother for a tour of the place, Iva Mae was happy to move. The staff had paid particular attention to her, so she immediately felt a connection to them. The facility was also affiliated with the Baptists, which she approved of. Sandy and Reggie and some friends moved her into the one-room apartment. Sandy once again decorated the small room with family photos, a collection of her plates from around the world, and other items that had sentimental value. Iva Mae was downsizing once again, and many items were now stored at Sandy's home. The room was small, so they put in a twin bed that was part of Sandy's trundle set. She had her recliner with a small table to use while she was either eating or writing. Next to it was her end table with her telephone, answering machine, and important contact information. She had a bookcase with a few books but mostly filled with family photos and gifts of miscellaneous items. The room had a very small dorm-type refrigerator and cabinet. The closet was a large cabinet that held her clothes and shoes and was very crowded, as Iva Mae still loved to shop and wear her jewelry when going out of the room for a meal or with Sandy. But Iva Mae's after-five attire was still her favorite outfit, and it had become her go-to clothing for comfort while in her room.

Iva Mae was using a wheelchair to get around by pushing herself with her legs. She also had a walker to use in her room to get herself back and forth to the bathroom. Over the years Sandy had organized her mother's life so that she was getting her Medicare and Medicaid. She also had many other programs under which Iva Mae received needed items without cost, including adult diapers. Sandy would go to all of Iva Mae's doctor's appointments with her because her mother would either not listen to what the doctor told her or forget the information. Iva Mae didn't mind the wheelchair too much, as it gave her the freedom to still get around, and using it was much easier than trying to walk. She still had Sandy to take care of all her shopping, outings, and doctor's appointment needs.

Her days were filled with getting up and having an orange or small snack while watching the news on television. She then got dressed if she felt like it and went to the dining room for lunch. She had made a few friends among the ladies who lived at the facility and would sit with them. She got great attention from the staff, especially the executive director, who often commented on Iva Mae's beautiful hair. It had turned completely white without the gray tinge. She would get it cut and occasionally have a little permanent added for a wave. Iva Mae liked to take care of how she looked and loved the attention she got for her trouble.

Iva Mae's aging process was beginning to show more as she approached the last year in her eighties. Over the years she had become less steady on her feet. Her daily routine started with getting up around eight o'clock in the morning and watching the news on television while fixing her orange and having her morning coffee before taking her medication. She would spend a little time reading the Bible, reading her mail, or answering a letter. Once she felt strong enough, she dressed for the day and looked forward to either Sandy stopping by for errands and appointments, which included lunch out, or eating in the dining room of the assisted-living facility.

The building was older and made of concrete blocks—clean, but still with the feeling of a nursing home rather than apartment living. Each resident had their own apartment and could decorate it as they wanted. As you walked through the building, some residents had their doors open and you could see the different lifestyles of the inhabitants inside. The main dining room was in the center of the complex. This was the hub of the organization, with a nurse's station, medication room, and the offices of the executive director and other staff members. Iva Mae loved the staff and the attention they gave her. They all talked about her beautiful white hair and teased her when she got it cut and said they wanted to get their hair done just like it. Iva Mae took great care of the way she looked. Her closet was full of outfits to wear, and she always made sure she had earrings to match. Sandy would still take her shopping occasionally to purchase a new blouse, shoes, or something that would give her mother enjoyment.

ROBIN ANNE GRIFFITHS

Chapter 47

The year 2012 had significant events worldwide. The beginning of the year had Queen Elizabeth celebrating her Diamond Jubilee. Iva Mae could remember the queen's coronation in 1953. The Mayan calendar was ending, and great speculation about whether the world would be ending was the buzz in the media. Early in the year the Midwest experienced deadly tornadoes, and later there was a mass shooting in Colorado. The price of gasoline was on the rise, and the economy was slowly recovering as the unemployment rate began to improve. The year was also full of events for Iva Mae's family, one in particular that was certainly not expected or planned.

Robin was getting married in May of that year. She knew her mother would not be able to attend but sent her an invitation: a scroll in a bottle as part of a pirate wedding theme. Iva Mae had little interest in the event since she would not be attending or be part of the attention. She worried about getting a gift for Robin and her new husband, Jim. Sandy told her not to be concerned, as she would take care of it. After the wedding Robin took the photos and video and made a short movie with music. Each family member who had attended received a copy, and Sandy took one over to her mother for a showing. Iva Mae appeared to be interested at first but quickly lost her concentration since she was not in the film. She also had great concerns because the wedding was not a Christian service and had a pirate theme with people in costume, which caused her to worry that the wedding wasn't real in God's eyes, or legal. Sandy was often irritated with her mother's reactions and narrow thoughts but continued to do what was needed.

At the end of the previous year, Reggie had become engaged, and Iva Mae was very excited because her grandson was getting married. At ninety, she was happy that she had met and liked Reggie's future wife, April. Iva Mae had worried for years about Reggie, if for no other reason than out of habit after his teenage years and growing pains moving into adulthood. She was happy that he was finally settling down. The wedding was set for October, and the family was once again planning to come in for the event. The wedding was to be held in Fort Worth at the historic YWCA. Plans for the rehearsal dinner, wedding, and hotel where the family would be staying were in the works, and Sandy was the main contact for all questions and concerns. Sandy was excited about the wedding but a little anxious about the family and juggling all the needs with the wedding couple's itinerary. About a month before the big day the schedule was pretty much in place.

The plan was for the members of the family and others in the wedding party to arrive before Thursday, October 25. The wedding rehearsal was to take place at the YWCA at five o'clock that afternoon. Then everyone would leave to go to Lone Star Park at Grand Prairie for the rehearsal dinner and horse races. The dinner, with a box to watch the races, was to be held in a private suite. The plans also included the traditional birthday celebration on Friday for Mike, Denny, and Tammy. The wedding then would take place on Saturday, October 27, at six in the evening.

Iva Mae was planning her wedding outfit with Sandy's help as well as the gift she would be giving the couple. She was busy telling all her friends and acquaintances about the wedding and how proud she was of her grandson. She knew she would be sitting up front in a special spot with Sandy at the wedding. Iva Mae was also excited because most of the family would be coming in for the event and she would be able to visit with her grandchildren and great-grandchildren. She was always looking forward to the next event that would bring her together with her family and put her in the spotlight where she could get special attention.

On Wednesday, October 17, a terrible shock was in store for everyone, including Iva Mae. Sandy had been feeling ill, and after a visit to a walk-in clinic the previous evening, she went home and passed away in her sleep. Her son, Reggie, found her the next morning when he stopped in with a little surprise breakfast. After trying to revive her and calling emergency services, he knew she was gone.

The phone calls afterward were upsetting, stunning, and distressing for all who knew and loved Sandy. Reggie and April went to see Iva Mae at her apartment that evening to tell her the news. Once they gave her the news, April remembers, "She just sat in her recliner and rocked. She didn't say anything, really. She didn't know what she was going to do because she was all alone now. We explained that she had all of us and that we'd help her. I don't think she was listening, because she just kept saying she didn't know what she was going to do." Iva Mae didn't cry in front of anyone. She now felt she was totally alone. She had counted on Sandy for as long as she could remember. Sandy was the strong one who could do anything she set her mind to doing. Iva Mae truly was afraid, because she had counted on Sandy for everything. She did not believe anyone could or would take care of her and all her needs. The staff and management at Iva Mae's facility were worried about her since she showed so little emotion over the death of her eldest daughter. They shared their concern with her family and paid a little extra attention to watch her and see if she was all right.

Robin left that evening to be at Reggie's side and help take care of whatever details needed looking after. Denny followed the next day. With the wedding ten days away, much needed to be accomplished. Robin and Denny were put in charge of going through Sandy's home and getting everything cleaned out. Sandy had always been a collector, but it had gotten out of hand during the previous several years. She had an incredible number of items to be packed up, given away, or trashed. Iva Mae was not brought to her house during the process. She was given updates on what was planned going forward and watched to make sure she felt included in what was going to happen next. Denny and Robin worked for several days on the house until Denny returned home. Robin planned to stay until the wedding and spent most of the time in Sandy's home going through a lifetime of memories as she continued to sort the items that needed to go. Tammy, Amber, and Michael with their children were in the process of moving into their new home, and they too were busy with packing and getting into the house. They brought the moving truck over to Sandy's and loaded up furniture and other items that they could use and needed. Robin set aside all the items that were keepsakes for Reggie to go through at another time. The process was exhausting and stressful for everyone.

As Sandy had always requested, she was cremated. It was decided that since the family was coming into town anyway, a celebration of Sandy's life would be held the Friday before the wedding. The rehearsal and dinner would still be on Thursday, and on Friday a room was rented for family and friends to join together to honor the life of Sandra Wyant. More than a hundred people came to pay respects, and there was standing room only as the family showed photos of her life and talked about who she was to them and how she had affected their life. Iva Mae was concerned and a little upset that there would not be a formal funeral with a pastor speaking, but she did speak during the ceremony. At the front of the room in her wheelchair at ninety years old, she talked about how much Sandy had meant to her and what she was like as a baby. She did not cry and was perhaps one of the few in the room who did not tear up during the memorial.

Sandy's obituary to sum up her life shared her overall accomplishments as well as gave a sense of the type of person she was and had become, but it could never give the depth of the support, friendship, and caring person she freely gave to others.

Sandra J. Wyant, age 63, railroader, crafter, and loving mother died unexpectedly at her home on Wednesday, October 17th.

She was born February 24th 1949 in Independence KS to Emerson and Iva Mae. Her earliest years were spent on both the family's farm and the little country general store in Oak Valley, Kansas. She moved to the Ozark Mountains and graduated from Parkview High School in Springfield, Missouri.

Her long and successful railroad career began with the Frisco Railroad in St. Louis and Springfield MO. Once merged with the Burlington Northern, she moved to positions with them in Birmingham, Alabama and San Bernardino, California. During her career, she reached the level of Yard Master and then was one of the first women to become a Train Master. She retired from the BNSF Railroad in Ft Worth, Texas. She met and married her husband, Donnie, a fellow railroader.

An avid crafter, Sandy filled the homes of friends and family with her creative gifts. She loved to travel highlighted by recent trips to the deltas of Viet Nam as well as the pursuit of Mt. Kilimanjaro and the Tanzania jungles. One of her greatest delights was being in the bleachers when her son Reggie participated in High

School sports.

Sandy is survived by her son, Reggie who followed her into a career with the railroad; her daughter Debi; three grandchildren, Grant, Emma, and Leo; her husband, Donnie; sisters Robin and Tammy; brother, Dennis, and her mother, Iva Mae. She is also survived by nieces, nephews, other relatives, many friends, and her about-to-be daughter-in-law, April. She was preceded in death by her father, Emerson. Sandy, always a lover of animals, rescued her dog and three cats. In lieu of flowers, Sandy would certainly have been appreciative of a contribution in her memory to your local Humane Society.

After the memorial was over and the room had cleared, the remaining family left to celebrate the October birthdays as they always had when together. The large group gathered at a restaurant to celebrate Denny's, Tammy's, and Mike's birthday, taking up almost an entire room at the Texas barbecue eatery. Cards were given to the birthday recipients, and photos that had been found while cleaning Sandy's home were passed around and given to any who wanted them for memories. The group talked about the hurricane that was striking the East Coast: Hurricane Sandy was the deadliest and most destructive hurricane of the year and the second-costliest one in the history of the United States. Even though the group was still in shock from the loss, they found the irony in the situation. Some felt that Sandy was angry that her plans had been interrupted. She had waited so long to be retired to travel more and enjoy her crafts. She was excited about the future with her son getting married and having his own family. She looked forward to being a part of their life. Sandy had a temper, and although she did not show it often, everyone stayed out of her way when she was angry. Under the circumstances, the hurricane had been named appropriately.

Chapter 48

The following day was the big day for Reggie and April. While they were busy with getting the last-minute details together, Denny and Robin helped with errands that Sandy would have done. Robin took Jim over to meet Iva Mae, and they had lunch. Iva Mae took great pride in telling Jim about Robin as a child, and her memory was excellent on the details. She was happy to finally meet Robin's new husband

and told Robin later that she could tell that Jim "liked her" since he came to have lunch with her and listen to her stories. She thought he was a nice man.

Robin had helped her mother pick out all her clothes and accessories for each of the events that week. Iva Mae appeared to be getting a few things confused, so Robin gathered all the outfits together and put the jewelry and shoes with each to help her. She assured her that all would be fine and that she, Denny, and Reggie would take care of her. Reggie and April had already decided and offered to step up to handle the responsibilities that Sandy had taken care of for so long. At the time, Tammy had said she would help where possible but made it clear that she would not be doing it all and preferred not to be involved if she wasn't needed. Iva Mae continued to be worried about who would take her to the doctor and handle the paperwork and all the other things she wasn't even sure about since Sandy had just done it all.

The day of the wedding was clear and beautiful—warm but not too hot. Robin and Jim had a rented van to transport the family from place to place. Robin was driving, but even with her GPS had difficulty, since the interstate construction was changing faster than the satellite updates. The group was to be at the YWCA at a specific time. From the hotel the group went to pick up Iva Mae at her apartment at the assisted-living facility. It took time to get her to the vehicle in the wheelchair and loaded. On the way to the YWCA, Robin took a wrong turn and had to backtrack. Iva Mae was nervous and anxious and began to worry. She got irritated with Robin and told her they were going to be late. She was not very nice in her comments and continued to tell Robin that they should have left earlier.

Iva Mae's grandchildren in the van were a little surprised at how she was acting, because she had never talked to them in that manner. She had always had a different—and better—relationship with them than she did with her children, particularly her daughters. Despite her worry, they made it to the wedding well before needed and spent the time meeting April's family and mingling with others while taking photos. Iva Mae still sat in the front row next to the empty seat that was to be for Sandy.

The wedding was held in an elegant setting of a great room with a large fireplace at the center where the couple took their vows. The ceramic tile floor and tall beamed and stenciled ceiling echoed the couple's words to each other. Iva Mae was proud to be there to watch her grandson, who gave his first smile to her as he became a husband and began a new life. Afterward, the reception and party was held upstairs in the grand ballroom, which had a wonderful marble staircase decorated with a wrought-iron railing. The room was beautifully set with arched windows enhanced with black-and-gold tapestry draperies. Fortunately the building was equipped with an elevator so Iva Mae was easily able to move from floor to floor. After dinner, toasting the couple, their first dance, and other ceremony customs, Denny and Robin gathered Iva Mae and took her back to her apartment. She was tired, as it had been a long day and late night for her. She was happy for Reggie but talked more about how she just didn't know what she was going to do without Sandy's help. Her son and daughter continued to reassure her that all would be fine.

Reggie and April left the next morning for their honeymoon. The family began to gather at the airport to make their way home. Tammy had been asked to help Iva Mae while Reggie was out of town, and the family thought she would be able to do it, but Amber had had an issue with the family at the wedding and was angry and hurt, so she and Tammy were putting the family at a distance once again. The previous several days had been difficult for everyone as they dealt with Sandy's death. Emotions were running high, and as always, Tammy felt like an outsider. Amber was feeling the same way.

Robin and Denny stayed in touch with Iva Mae while Reggie and April were gone and talked often with the executive director of the assisted-living facility to make sure she was getting what she needed. Denny contacted the director to thank her for the attention she was giving to their mother. Iva Mae would talk often about how, in spite of all her aches, pains, and medical problems, she was in the best place she'd lived in decades. It was comforting to know what good care she was getting from the staff. The director responded, saying, "WOW! Thank you so very much. She is dear to us all, and, well, with the loss of her Sandy, we are just trying to fill in some shoes where we can. Iva Mae is really a dear, dear person, and it makes me smile to know we are making her life more comfortable. Thank you for the note."

Reggie and April came back from their honeymoon and began to live the life of a married couple. They began to build a home together, and while the construction was going on, Reggie took his grandmother to see the property. The house was at the bottom of a very steep hill, and Iva Mae did not think she would be able to go down to see it even with her wheelchair. Reggie asked some of the construction workers if they would help carry her so she could see the home. They did, and Iva Mae bragged to all her family and friends about the adventure. Reggie had always been special to her, and now he was "the favorite," as Robin would tease him.

Tammy had begun with good intentions to help where she could, although her gut told her this would not work. She and Amber planned to have Iva Mae over for Thanksgiving that year, including a big dinner with all the food Iva Mae liked.

Tammy wrote Robin an email about the upcoming day:

> We are trying to go through everything we own and the other stuff from the move. It is a difficult job. There are so many boxes that things are just buried. This weekend we will clean up the house and look at getting more out of the garage. We have talked to Mom about Thanksgiving. I will take some medication to make it through the day. I think we will get a turkey from the grocery store. Amber will make hot rolls and cinnamon rolls. I have a potato cheese recipe that a woman at work makes that is really good. Then round it out with what vegetables we can get the children, Mom, and Amber to eat. Oh, and we will make pumpkin pies. That is the plan so far.

It was disappointing for Tammy but not surprising that her mother was not very complimentary or thankful about the meal or the time spent with them. Iva Mae was still on the quest to fix Tammy to be more like the Treadways and not like her father, Bob. The day was not happy for either one of them, but they did not argue. They ended up taking Iva Mae back to her apartment as soon as the meal was over, as she was tired.

In December Tammy planned again to have her mother over for Christmas. She knew that of all the holidays, Christmas was her mother's favorite, and she felt obligated to do what was expected. Tammy's health was not good, and in fact it was beginning to deteriorate and she was missing a lot of work and spending more time at medical appointments. Her words to Robin about the holiday were "I have to call Mom to get her set up for Christmas. We are not happy to have her over, but Reggie has made plans. She will have to suck it up this year."

Reggie still had a lot hanging over his head with settling Sandy's affairs and taking on the responsibility of Iva Mae. The couple did their best to get her to doctor's appointments and take her out as often as possible. At one point Reggie was with her at a doctor's appointment and had to help her get dressed. To say the least, it was a difficult assignment for a young man of twenty-nine to be the caregiver of his ninety-year-old grandmother.

Tammy was still participating some with Iva Mae's care but only if she absolutely needed to be a part of the process as reflected in the email she sent to Robin and Denny:

> Mom is going to the doctor on Friday. I have asked for a float vacation day and am going to go with her. She is supposed to get the cyst drained off the back of her knee. The nurse at her facility said that it probably would come back periodically; I am going to ask the doctor. I am also going to find out about the medication lists and the allergic lists. Other than that I am open to suggestions on what needs to be done if anything. If you want me to find out anything, please let me know. I was usually good with Mom in the past; it was just the stress on me that is the problem. I will be taking meds though.

Robin and Denny called their mother often. Robin would send out emails to family and friends, giving reports on Iva Mae and encouraging everyone to call her as often as possible or to send her cards and letters. Denny and Robin planned to visit her in July, not long after Iva Mae's birthday, to check on what they could do to help her and, they hoped, take a little burden off the others. Before their trip, Tammy was asked to help with an appointment but told Robin that she could not do it with her busy schedule. She resented the request to call her mother or have her daughter and grandchildren involved. This led to a disagreement between her and Reggie and a complete and final break between them, and marked the end of her seeing her mother.

The resentment over the years had grown to the point that Tammy could no longer take the pressure of her mother. She wrote her thoughts about the situation in an email to Robin:

I try to pay it forward. I just don't include Mom in the mix. I look at her and I see her face telling me that I will never be anything, that I am fat and worthless. I see every time she slapped me, or threw something in my face. How she would follow me around the house screaming at me and trying to hit whatever she could. I see the woman that told me that I had better get an education because no man would put up with me and my health issues so I would always be on my own. The same woman that told Amber over and over that I was not a fit mother and she felt sorry for her that she was my daughter. I know that people look at her and see a kindly faced old woman. I see a twisted face of misery that is not content unless she is the center of attention and is making others know how important she is, and is waiting to drag someone down. For me it is way too late to build any relationship, or for me to feel anything for her.

I put up with her way too many years because I had the impression that it was something you had to do. Then I realized that you do not have to keep people in your life that make you miserable. If you have to take anti-anxiety medication just to talk to someone, let alone see them, they don't need to be in your life.

These years in Texas have been a struggle for me concerning Mom. On one hand I hate Mom and my stomach churns whenever I see her. I struggle with every moment around her. Then there is the loyalty to my brothers and sisters that expect me to be a part of the family and help them with the old biddy.

The next problem after that is I didn't bring Mom to Texas, Sandy did. I didn't want to be anywhere around her. When I was in Topeka, I did not call her or visit her. Sorry, but I really didn't. Then she is here and I am trying to help Sandy because she drove Sandy nuts. Then Sandy dies. I thought I made it clear then that I wanted nothing to do with her. I thought that you or Denny would make arrangements to take her to Florida. I know that you didn't want to, but I did not want to either. I thought I made it very clear that I was not interested in taking care of her and being in her life.

Next thing I know, Reggie said he would take care of it, and he being almost thirty, I figured okay, let him volunteer. Now I feel like people are trying to drag me back into her life. I know it is selfish of me, but I don't want to be in her life. I resent it. I get emails from you and Denny on what to do about Mother. Reggie took that over, not me. About the only thing I want to know about

Mom is when to go say goodbye to her and about the funeral. I know it is cold. I am cold about her. I know this probably sounds hurtful, but I cannot pull out feelings I don't have. It takes everything I have just to talk to her without being rude.

Iva Mae at 90 years old

Chapter 49

R eggie and April decided to treat Iva Mae to an outing
to get her nails done for her birthday. This was not an
easy task, as they had to call around the area to find an
English-speaking person who was white because they knew
that Iva Mae would have a hard time understanding someone
with an accent plus she had become more prone to saying
things out loud that came from her upbringing and were not
politically correct. This was also a week or so after celebrity

chef Paula Deen had gotten in trouble for using racial slurs.

Before they left Iva Mae's assisted-living facility, Reggie had a
talk with his grandmother about saying the wrong things while
they were out in case they ran into any black people. They had
found a place by the mall and scheduled an appointment.
Things were going great while they were getting their
manicures. Iva Mae was very pleased with all the compliments
about her hair and how she didn't look ninety-one years old.
About that time a little girl around five years old, who appeared
to be biracial, black and white, came running in to talk to the
woman doing Iva Mae's nails. Reggie and April were
immediately on edge, hoping she remembered "the talk" they'd
had an hour before. Their grandma was on her best behavior,
but when they got to the car, she said proudly, "See, I didn't
say the N-word!" She had a great time showing off her
manicure when she returned to the assisted-living home and
bragged to all the people there about her wonderful family and
how they took care of her.

Before Robin and Denny arrived to visit their mother, she was
calling each of them to complain about headaches that would
not go away. Iva Mae had always been vocal about anything
that bothered her, but this was a little more than usual. Reggie
let Robin know that he had had to put parental control on her
cell phone because she had unknowingly downloaded some
applications. She had had the phone from Sandy for the last
several years to carry with her in case she needed it. The phone
was like most technology for Iva Mae: she didn't understand it
or want any part of it, but she kept it because she was told she
might need it to call.

As part of the trip, Robin and Denny planned to take her to

her doctor and find out what was causing the headaches. When they arrived, they found she was showing signs of memory problems. She was a little more disconnected than previously. She was excited to see them and eager to visit. She was still complaining about the headaches and also her feet hurting. Denny and Robin took her to her doctor, who believed she might have had a stroke and that that was the cause of the headaches. He did not seem overly concerned and overall led them to believe there was not much that could be done because of her age. At ninety-one she was showing more signs of aging than ever before.

The trip out of the assisted-living facility that day included a doctor visit, shopping for shoes, and a barbecue lunch. Iva Mae ate little and was tired quickly. Although she was in a wheelchair, her feet bothered her a lot. She had had terrible bunions that over the years had become much worse and caused some of her toes to cross. She reminded Robin that her sister Lula had had the same problem but even more so, with several toes overlapping each other. Once they returned to her apartment, Denny and Robin worked with her on her phone messaging machine. She told them that she could not get it to work. They purchased a new one and set it up for her to learn how to use it. It was a simple machine, but Iva Mae could not remember which buttons to push to listen and delete the messages. This little change was huge for her children to witness, as she had never displayed confusion of this magnitude. It was obvious that something was wrong.

Denny left for home a couple of days before Robin, who helped her by cleaning her apartment and going through boxes and items she no longer wanted or needed. They went through all the items in her closet, and Iva Mae talked about many of the outfits that Sandy had bought her and how much she missed her. Robin helped her mother address several letters to friends to whom she wanted to send an article with a note. Iva Mae was having trouble concentrating on writing.

Before her headache episode Iva Mae had written a life history that she was going to present to her church gathering at the assisted-living facility. The small group met in one of the common rooms each Sunday with a preacher who came in to talk to them about their lesson for the week. They had asked her to talk about her life this coming Sunday. She was prepared with several handwritten pages.

> I am no speaker. I was the last child. Mom and Dad had nine children. The first, one son, then two daughters, then three children, girls, but they all died. Then my two brothers followed by me. I was the last and weighed ten pounds. I was born before the Fourth of July and they all called me a Fourth of July baby.

> I was about nine when my mom took sick. She was operated on, and when I was older, she really took sick. We all thought she had cancer. She got worse, and when I was fifteen in June, she told me to call all the kids to come home. I went up to the store and called. They all came home except my brother Raymond was late. Soon he drove up and Mom had been laughing and telling about Raymond and I fighting that morning. His car wouldn't start and he wanted me to drive his car. I did but drove it off in the ditch. Everyone but Lula and I went to meet Raymond and Mom was just laughing. Then all at once she gasped and died. I know Mom went to heaven. God had told her it was time. She was fifty-four.

I was rather on my own or had to be on my own for the summer. So in the fall of my senior year my good friend and I went to Altamont to school. It was a good one. We took our senior year and also took a course studying teaching. We took them both and passed. I was sixteen. We both got schools in Elk County. I found a family to stay with and I taught four years. My dad then died. He had gone to Parsons to stay with my sister.

I then met a friend through some other friends. He had never been married but he had a good farm with a house, and he was also twenty-nine years older than me. I was nineteen years old and I needed a home. So we were married in Kansas City. His two sisters lived in Kansas City. We lived in Howard, Kansas. But he taught me cooking, cleaning, and taking care of chickens, gathering eggs, how to fry chickens, garden, ride horses, drive a car, tractor, and more. He even taught me how to make home brew. We had beer parties and lots of company.

We had a son and his dad thought he was wonderful. He would go to parties with us. The war was going on and we had our second baby, Sandy. I lost Sandy a few months ago.

Em (their dad) had been in the war and he was getting tired. We sold our farm and bought a store and it had a post office about twenty-five miles from where we were. I took over the post office. After we were there three years and Em was still drinking, I left. He got a divorce. I went to Kansas City and got a job in an oil company.

I worked three years and met another guy. I thought he was nice but I was fooled. He worked for the railroad and we married. We had Robin, and then I got pregnant again, which he didn't like. I was sick a lot. He got some medicine for me I thought was from my doctor but it wasn't. It was from an animal doctor and it made me sick. I needed to go to the hospital but he wouldn't take me so Denny took me. He was mad at me. He put salt in my bed and other things, then took a knife to my throat. He was holding Tammy, so Robin, who was five, had to run to her aunt's (my sister's) home down the road and told them to come help.

Tammy was sick and she had to have surgery. She works for the railroad now and she has had quite a time all her life.

I tried to get a divorce but they told me I couldn't because he wasn't okay. Well, I put up with him. He got the sheriff to put a sign up so we couldn't get in the house. I went to a judge. He told me to go to Springfield and we could get a policeman. We did.

I told my sister I was going to get a three-bedroom house with a fenced backyard with a school and go to church. I had made up my mind I needed Jesus. I was thinking all the time I needed him. The first house I found was perfect. It had three bedrooms, a backyard that was fenced, and a church just down the street with a school across from it. It was inexpensive, and my Sunday school teacher lived next door. He and his wife had a daughter, and their grandchildren were the ages of Robin and Tammy. Then my best friend lived behind me down the street. We are still best friends. Of course I had to put up with Bob. He didn't have a job so I had to work. I picked up kids to watch and other jobs. Whatever I could do to make money I did.

The kids loved it. Denny was in college, Sandy was in high school, and Robin was starting grade school. Tammy was just getting ready to start kindergarten. The first morning we went to church we came home and Bob and three other men were sitting drinking at the table. I went to the table and threw it all away. The second Sunday Sandy and I went up and were saved. I had stopped drinking. I really stopped. I didn't want anything but God. I stopped cussing too. Even in two days. I didn't even want to tell dirty jokes or anything like I did before. But I had wondered if I did it right. I prayed and prayed if I did it okay and was really saved. One night I was dreaming in bed and I thought Jesus was over me in the bed and was beckoning me to come up. I was yelling, "I am coming, I am coming," and I woke up everyone in the house. I never worried again. I have had Jesus all the time.

A pastor helped me to get a divorce. Bob got married again. He needed someone to feed him but he didn't live long.

My life has been good after I moved into another home. Then I went to Washington, DC, to be with my son and be in charge of his two boys for five years. Afterward I went to St. Louis and helped with Sandy's boy and Tammy's girl. We had fun. I got to travel a lot: Europe, Hawaii, New York, Niagara Falls, and many other places.

I finished working after ten years with Kmart, then helped in the hospital for fifteen years volunteering. Then I had a back operation, so Sandy and Reggie moved me to Texas and here I am today. I have loved my kids.

Robin hated to leave her mother that Sunday morning. She knew that her mother's aging process had taken a big turn and expected things to become harder to handle and more difficult.

Chapter 50

After the visit from Robin and Denny, Iva Mae began to have more problems. She had to be taken to the hospital and was admitted. Many tests were given but without a definite outcome to apply a strategy. Once admitted, Iva Mae took a turn for the worse. She would have good and bad days, but even the good were full of confusion.

Reggie and April scheduled physician appointments to see

what could be done to help her. April worked for a physician and was a true blessing in Iva Mae's life, as she was able to navigate the medical system with more ease. This email from April describes some of her efforts to help:

> I've scheduled an appointment for Iva Mae to see a neuro-ophthalmologist for this upcoming Monday morning to see if he can do anything for her vision. Also, my boss looked at some of her meds and said that he thought there were some unneeded things on there for someone of her age, but he hasn't ever seen her either. From what we can tell, it looks like everything that would affect her memory are things she was on before, but it's kind of hard to tell because the med list we have has a start date listed from the day she was discharged from the hospital. He also said that it's common for people who've had a stroke to have good days and bad days, memory wise. I talked to Iva Mae yesterday and her hips and legs were hurting. I talked to the nurse and she was going to have the doctor go in and see her. They said they could give her medication and heating packs, but didn't know if she would take the meds. Reggie called up there and talked her into it, but I haven't been able to get ahold of her this morning to see how she's feeling. We're going to run by there tonight before we go to dinner to grab her dirty laundry and check on her.

Later April continued the conversation:

Here's the rundown on what happened at the appointment this morning. They couldn't really do an eye exam because Iva Mae couldn't tell them what the letters or pictures were. She could see them, but couldn't come up with the words to explain what they were. The doctor dilated her eyes and said everything looked good from his point of view. He didn't think there was anything wrong with her eyes, but more her mental capabilities and trying to explain what she is seeing. He said the eyes will usually adjust back to normal about a week after the stroke. He said he was very concerned about her mental status though and said that she needs to get in with a neurologist. I've left a message with her physician's office to send a referral to the neuro doctor she saw in the hospital. This way he already knows what's going on and hopefully we can get her in faster since she's sort of already established with him. We schedule a follow-up visit with the ophthalmologist for two months from now.

Iva Mae ended up back in the hospital, then moved into a rehabilitation center. Robin sent out an email to the family members:

Hi everybody. I just wanted to keep you up to date about Mom. She was put into the hospital last week for an infected foot plus some stomach issues. They did a scope and found a few things like ulcers. She has had her meds changed and they are treating her foot. She may have to have surgery on it but they are working on trying to fix it without having to operate. She is getting vague about what is going on and we have all decided that she needs to go into a nursing facility. She has tried to leave the rehab center a couple of times and at the hospital she has pulled her IV out a few times. The phone is too hard for her to get to at the hospital and she is really not answering it anyway. Reggie will call me when he is there and puts her on the phone but she really doesn't want to talk much.

She has good and bad days. Reggie and April are working with a friend that is a social worker to place her into the best place we can that will be close to them so they can watch over her. They are going on a trip next month and I will be going to Texas to be with her and help with the organization of some of her stuff that she currently has at the assisted-living place.

All of Iva Mae's life she had enjoyed talking with her family and friends on the phone. Now she might answer, or she might not. Her children decided that perhaps the mobile phone was the problem and had a phone installed in her room to make it easier for her to take calls. It did not help. When she did talk to someone, she would say that the staff were laughing at her or making fun of her. Sometimes when Robin called, she would answer and tell her that she didn't feel good, and would cry a little. When asked if she was eating, she would answer, "If they bring anything." Her family kept encouraging her to work at doing what they told her to do to get better so she could return to her apartment.

It was finally determined that Iva Mae had had a stroke and it was causing dementia. Although different with each individual, it was coming on fast for her, and she was becoming less of herself each day. She was losing her appetite and weight. Her foot was improving, but she was showing signs of depression. She would wander in her wheelchair and even was able to escape the facility out into a busy road. The staff then decided this was not the place for her and that she needed more supervision. Reggie and April kept a close eye on her and visited her often. It was difficult, as her clothes, shoes, and other items would just disappear. They began the search for a nursing home since it had become clear that she would not be returning to the assisted-living apartment. Reggie and April worked to find a place that would take her since she was on both Medicare and Medicaid. It was not easy and took a great deal of time and research to find a place that was acceptable and would admit her.

It was October 2013, a year after Sandy's death. An acceptable nursing home was found, and although it was not too close to Reggie and April's house, it was clean and the staff appeared to care and be attentive. Reggie and April left for a well-deserved vacation, and Robin and Nancy flew in to help with the transition from Iva Mae's apartment to the nursing home. The first day, they both went to visit her at the nursing home. It was a typical home with many elderly people sitting in the halls with aides and nursing staff moving people to different locations.

Robin was shocked when she saw her mother. She appeared a little disheveled, and her hair was much longer than usual. She was unable to get out of the wheelchair by herself and had to be lifted in and out of her bed by the staff. She had to wear an adult diaper and a catheter bag for her urine. She barely talked, and Robin was not sure if Iva Mae recognized her. She had brought her ice cream, knowing that was her favorite food. Iva Mae didn't say too much, and it seemed difficult for her to speak. It appeared that she had trouble feeding herself, so Robin talked to her about family and other things while feeding her the ice cream. She appeared to be listening and understanding most of what she was hearing.

Robin was heartbroken to see her mother in this place and condition. She shared a room with another resident. She had a bed, a nightstand, and a wardrobe closet with the bare minimum of clothes. She had no jewelry on, and her clothes looked worn and old. The room was bare of her family photos other than a couple of items. Her Bible was in her nightstand but did not appear to have been touched. She knew her mother's greatest fears had come true: she was in a nursing home and did not have all her faculties. The day after Robin and Nancy visited Iva Mae at the nursing home, she was taken to the hospital, as she was not doing well. She remained there the entire week that Robin and Nancy were in town. The days were filled with driving to her apartment and clearing out all her personal items, then driving to the hospital to visit and sit with her.

Both Robin and Nancy worked all week cleaning out the apartment and gathering all the things that needed to be kept. Many items were given away, such as the seventy packages of adult diapers that Nancy found and gathered onto a flatbed cart. They had been stored away in every corner possible in the small room. Robin found her mother's most important metal box where she kept all her important papers. Robin knew that her mother would be happy to know it was safe. Denny suggested and Robin agreed that they needed to put together a bag for Reggie and April in case she passed away so they would be prepared for her to be taken to the funeral home. Robin found her favorite "after-five attire" and set it aside for them to have when needed. At one point Robin thought for sure that her mother was not going to make it and that she would go while she was there. She even told her mother at the hospital that it was okay to let go. She was there to take care of her.

In the evenings Nancy and Robin would go through her keepsakes. Robin opened the metal box and was surprised at the findings. Iva Mae's life came out of the metal box and began to tell a story of who she was and what was special to her. Cards from her children, baby teeth, and hair clippings were among the items. Her wishes for her funeral and her written obituary were included. Special photographs, her Social Security card, and other personal objects were in the small box. It was like opening a time capsule in a small box.

The week went quickly, and soon it was time for both Robin and Nancy to go home. Nancy left first and Robin had a couple of days to finalize the remainder of the things needing to be done with the assisted-living apartment and her status at the nursing home. The first thing she did was take a few of her mother's favorite framed photos to her room and hang them up. She also added a few decorative items to cheer up the bland room.

She hated leaving her mother in the hospital and spent the last day there sitting with her and trying to talk to her when she wasn't sleeping. Robin realized how truly beautiful her mother was at that moment. Her skin was porcelain, and even at ninety her wrinkles were not deep lines. Her hair was a bright white rather than gray, and her eyes were a clear, beautiful blue. They still had a laugh in them, and even now she enjoyed the nursing staff when they showed her attention. Robin gave her fragile mother a hug and kiss, knowing that it was probably the last time she would see her alive. She left the room, went to her car to go the airport, and sat and cried.

Reggie and April returned that evening, and about a week later Iva Mae improved and returned to the nursing home. A month later, on a Saturday, Robin received a call from the home that her mother was not doing well and they were contacting an ambulance to take her to the hospital. Robin had a feeling this was the end and prayed that God would take her so she would be at rest. It was time. She called Reggie to let him know about the call, and about fifteen minutes later, he called back to tell her that she was gone.

The family was notified and the planning began to see her last wishes taken care of in the way she wanted as much as possible.

It was mid-November, and the family made arrangements to have Iva Mae buried next to her family in Labette, Kansas. The funeral home transported her body from Texas to Kansas, and Reggie and April drove up in an ice storm to see that she was taken care of properly. The next plan was to have a memorial service in her hometown of Springfield on Saturday, December 7, so her friends and family could gather to pay tribute to her. Everyone made arrangements to meet there the day before the service. That Friday was Reggie's thirtieth birthday, so a little celebration was given that evening at a restaurant where the family gathered. The day before everyone arrived, Springfield had the worst storm it had seen in decades. It snowed, but ice was the biggest problem. Despite the weather, the family arrived without incident.

An obituary was put into the Springfield paper to let those who knew Iva Mae know about the service.

Iva Mae Hodge, 91, longtime resident of the Hurley-

Springfield, MO area, died peacefully on November 16, 2013 in Justin, TX. Born in Labette, KS on July 3, 1922, she was an active church member, a rural school teacher, postmaster, retired K-Mart-ER, quilter, mother, grandmother, great-grandmother and Lady Bears fan. She was a hospital volunteer for fifteen years. Preceded in death by her daughter, Sandra Wyant, she is survived by daughters, Robin Griffiths and Tammy Hodge; son, Dennis Wyant; six grandchildren; seven great-grandchildren and a host of family and friends. A celebration of her life is planned for Saturday, December 7, 2013 at 1:00 pm in Springfield, Missouri.

The service was at a funeral home just on the outskirts of town in a lovely chapel. It sat atop a hill by itself without any other buildings around. Robin, with Jim, had put together a video with photos of Iva Mae, from her childhood throughout her life. The video included some of her favorite hymns and music from the forties' big band era. Because of the weather the attendance was disappointing, but most of her best friends did manage to get to the service.

Denny began the tribute to his mother. Jane had made and brought Iva Mae's famous chocolate chip cookies to help everyone remember how wonderful she was in the kitchen. Her children and grandchildren spoke about what she meant to them. Tammy and her family did not attend.

Cousin Tim was asked to sing a song, as was the assistant pastor of her Springfield church. Then the pastor of the church talked about her faith and gave a quick sermon. Iva Mae would have been happy to know that through him she had one last chance to reach her family about Jesus.

Her friends spoke about her love of life, faith, sense of humor, and true friendship. Ultimately Iva Mae's long life and experiences were summed up by saying she was a hard worker who loved her family and had great faith in her God. She may have had fears, but they did not stop her from experiencing life. She accepted most of what life had given her and overall, looked for what she could take from each experience to move forward. She did not let the circumstances of the moment stop her from finding some humor in it and laugh, even if it wasn't worthy or appropriate. Although she may not always have been the best to her children, she did instill a drive to reach for more, explore possibilities, and not just settle. She believed she had done her best under the circumstances.

After the service, the family went to their cousin Tim and Sally's home for a meal and time together before everyone would leave the following day. Their home was out in the country in the hills of the Ozarks, and the ground was covered white with snow. A warm fire was burning, and the family sat around the table in the beautiful home, telling stories about the domineering matriarch of their family. Although Iva Mae had been difficult and always centered on herself, the conversation was about funny little stories of interaction with the individuals around her at different periods of her life.

While there, Robin went into a bedroom to check her phone. Reggie and April had driven up to the service from Texas and were already on their way back in the treacherous weather. April had left a text message that said she had forgotten to tell Robin that a few days before Iva Mae had passed away, she had told April, "Robin is very pretty, and I know that she loves me." Robin sat on the end of the bed in that room and cried. She cried because she had lost the person who had known her longer than anyone else. She cried because her mother was no longer a part of her life. She also laughed inside, knowing that her mother would have loved the attention she had received that day, although she also would have been disappointed that she was not there to bask in the glow of the moment.

Robin smiled through her tears and could feel that her mother was ultimately looking down upon the day and thinking, *They liked me.*

ROBIN ANNE GRIFFITHS

Epilogue

After Iva Mae's passing, Tammy's health continued to decline, and she spent much of 2014 in the hospital and a rehabilitation center for a serious staph infection that had required surgery. Her recovery was slow at best. Her diabetes continued to take her sugar levels on a roller coaster ride even with medication. She had great regrets about how her relationship with Sandy had ended and missed her sister and lifelong friend. She did not have any regrets about the end of her relationship with her mother.

For years she had been trying to get disability benefits so she could stay home and take care of herself. She did not like her job, and her quick mind and tongue continued to get her in trouble at work. After the surgery she finally received the disability benefits that she had wanted for so long. She lived with her daughter, Amber, and Amber's family took care of her. She could not drive safely, so her daughter took her wherever she needed to go. Staff members from medical home care visited her to manage her care, and Tammy had plans for what she wanted to do once she was better.

She talked to Robin every few weeks about her health, the grandchildren, and what she was going to do once she was financially able. Their relationship had become closer, and they finally understood that they were each different and it was okay. The Saturday after Memorial Day in 2015, Tammy called Robin and they talked for much longer than usual. After they ended the call, Robin was upset, as she didn't like the tone of the conversation or the way Tammy sounded.

The next evening Robin received the call that her sister, who was only fifty-four, had passed away. Robin immediately scheduled a flight for Texas to help Amber with arrangements. A memorial service was scheduled for June 4. Tammy was buried in a cemetery near Fort Worth with a stone that has two flying pigs on it—a favorite of hers. Tammy had collected many flying pigs over the years that began with a gift from Sandy.

Robin summed up her life with the following, which she read at the service:

Life goes on . . .

There are moments in life that we take for granted and then moments that bring us clarity. This is a time that I have been seeing both. In the last three years I have lost two sisters and my mother. With each passing I have been taught lessons that I hope will be with me always. Last month I wrote an article talking about cherished moments. Today I want to expand on those thoughts.

My sister Tammy passed away May 31. She was born in 1960. It was the beginning of a new age and generation. As a country we were expanding our horizons and looking out to new adventures. Tammy was born with a birth defect, and from the moment she came into this world, she was at a disadvantage physically. She took it all in stride and became the different one in the family. She was incredibly smart. I believe she was the most intelligent person I have ever known. She was reading books well in advance of her age in grade school. She questioned everything and followed her own path with the confidence that I never had or understood. She had a sense of adventure, and when she was younger, explored caves with a group of students for science. Tammy would look for the outrageousness of thought and gravitate to that philosophy. She had an opinion on everything and usually had an interesting perspective even if you disagreed. Many don't know this, but Tammy was very emotional and sensitive. Growing up she learn to hide her fear and retreat into her own world of books and the stories that she could control. Although I know there were many times she was afraid or worried, she usually had an attitude that all would be taken care of and others would be there to help her if she needed them. Her most precious gift in life was her daughter, Amber.

Tammy and Amber lived with me many years ago when Tammy was going to Clemson University. She worked a full-time job while attending school full time. I helped with getting Amber back and forth to day care, but Tammy really did all that was needed to make it work. She loved learning and actually wrote a book several years ago. We didn't always agree on things, but we found a way to get along and love each other as sisters do. Once she was very upset with me and told me that she wanted a sister more than she wanted to be angry. I have kept those words close to me for several years now as a motto of what is really important.

Tammy had been ill for a very long time. I was grateful when she finally got her full disability and did not have to work. Over the years her health had been deteriorating. We would talk fairly often, and she seldom dwelled on her issues other than when I pushed for details or she would make a joke out of it. She was more likely to talk about her family or the latest railroad drama that she was having. Tammy had a sense of humor. She could take the smallest detail and point out a humorous aspect. There were times we would laugh so hard that we both would be crying. She was not mechanically inclined. I taught her how to drive her first stick-shift car, and I wish YouTube had been around then, as I believe it would have been a top-rated funny video for the world to see. We had many moments like that, and I know that she had my back

many times when I was going through something painful.
Other times when we disagreed, she was honest and
direct. She had no problem letting me know how she felt.
Although that was sometimes painful, I always knew
where she stood.

The Saturday before she passed away, she called me and
we had a very long conversation. She was on a lot of
medication and having breathing problems, so at times it
was a little hard to understand her, but we did talk for a
long time. We talked about her health, but we also
touched on past experiences, funny moments, and shared
memories. Somehow I think she knew, and I was very
worried too. The day she passed away I had an emotional
moment about her that I even mentioned to my husband,
Jim. I believe that may have been the time she passed on
to a better place. She is no longer suffering, as she was in
a lot of pain these last few years. We are the ones who
must continue on without her. We can think about all the
"I could've . . . should've . . . would've . . . ," but we need
to know that life goes on and our memories of those who
mean the most to us must be treasured now.

So as we miss and remember the loved ones of our life,
we must focus on the things we can do to keep the people
we love close to us. I will miss her and her crazy outlook
on life. Most of all I will miss her funny sense of humor. I
try to think that we all have issues and difficulties and
look for the good that will be remembered. Let's create
the best memories possible as we move forward in life.

If Tammy were here and listening to this, she would
agree, then find the irony and humor and comment on it.

It would be thought-provoking as well as funny. So smile and remember all the good things that Tammy gave us in this life. I am grateful to have had her in my life. She was loved and she will be missed.

A Final Thought

Life doesn't wait for anything or anyone. It's fleeting and in constant motion. You can lose a loved one, experience failure or success, lose everything, or win big, but life does not stop. It's what we do from the moment we are born to the day we pass on that is important. Living a worthwhile life is what we should strive for as a goal. There is a poem called "The Dash," by Linda Ellis, and the content of the poem is about looking at a person's gravestone and the dash between the date they were born and the date they passed away. That dash represents their entire life and how they lived. The poem reminds us that our material possessions are not what are important but how we lived and loved and spent our time. That time is what is significant.

We have an opportunity to reach out to the world and do things that will make a difference in another's life. We can walk a path that is teaching us lessons. We take the experiences we have learned, the heartaches, hardships, loves, losses, successes, and achievements that in the end help make us a stronger person. It really is a choice we make every day. Choose to appreciate the people around you and live a life in accordance with your values and ideals.

A recent article suggested looking at your life as if you were in a movie. You are the star and director. You get to choose the story and how it will end. Will you make a movie that people enjoy, that they feel good watching, and that makes them happy because it ends well? The point is your life is the movie and you can make it into anything you choose. It can be an adventure, a love story, a family epic. A blockbuster! It is your choice.

We should savor all the joys and sorrows, and all the happiness and sadness we experience each day. We should appreciate our life and all that happens around it, because life goes on. Be mindful of the present moment.

In three words I can sum up everything I've learned about life: it goes on.

—**Robert Frost**

The End

From the author

The three years after my mother's death have been a learning experience. From the moment I opened Iva Mae's metal box of keepsakes and important papers, I knew I needed to write her story. It was a way of healing and coming full circle. I was looking for who she really was as a person and not just a mother. Once I began to write about her, I became inspired. I realized that we are all trying to do the best we can with what we have to work with and that we can

357

also choose to reach beyond our fears and step outside of our comfort zone. Iva Mae was not a perfect person by any means, but she lived life and did her best as she saw it. I am grateful that I had her in my life to learn from and see how her influence is part of who I am today.

I am thankful that I had such wonderful help putting this book together with memories from so many who added stories, notes, and comments to give the overall view of my mother's life. I could not have done it without the help of my brother, Dennis, as well as Judy, Reggie, April, Amber, Debi, Sally, Tim, Nancy, Dean, Donnie and the multitude of friends who contributed memories. I was also fortunate to have stories that many of her family members wrote about her over the years as well as the wonderful memories and diaries she kept and shared with us all. I am grateful to my dear friend Laurel, who edited this project. Her feedback has been invaluable. Most of all I want to thank my husband, Jim, who has been with me through so many emotions during a time of great loss. His support and patience has meant more than I can possibly describe in a few words.

Finally I would like to share with you my mother's chocolate chip cookie recipe that her family so enjoyed. A cookbook was assembled many years ago of all her favorite recipes. Sandy took each of our mother's handwritten recipes, typed them, then copied and put them into a folder. Each family member received their copy, and as new members came into the family, a book was given to them. There are probably a hundred recipes for breads, main dishes, and desserts as well as her holiday treats.

In the front of the cookbook she wrote the following:

Dear Family,

I hope you enjoy this cookbook as much as I enjoy cooking. Your recipes may not taste just like mine because no two cooks that use the same recipe turn out the same taste. I never measure accurately and do a lot of guessing. Some things I have never measured but did a lot of tasting. I love you all, MOM

Mrs. Wiley's Chocolate Chip Cookies

½ lb. oleo
1 cup white sugar
1 cup brown sugar
2 eggs
½ tsp. salt
½ tsp. baking powder
1 tsp. soda
1 tsp. vanilla
2 cups flour
2 cups quick cook oats
1 - 12 oz. package chocolate chips

Cream oleo and sugars. Add eggs and vanilla, mix. Then add flour, salt, baking powder, soda—mix well. Add oats and chocolate chips—mix. Drop by teaspoon onto greased cookie sheet and bake at 350 degrees about 10 min.

Enjoy.